Building Mobile Apps with React Native: Develop Apps for iOS and Android

A Step-by-Step Guide to Cross-Platform Mobile Development with React Native

BOOZMAN RICHARD

BOOKER BLUNT

Table of Content

TABLE OF CONTENTS

INTRODUCTION

Welcome to **"Mastering React Native: From Beginner to Expert"**, your ultimate guide to learning React Native and building high-quality mobile applications for both iOS and Android platforms. Whether you're a beginner eager to dive into mobile development or an experienced developer looking to expand your skills with React Native, this book is designed to equip you with everything you need to start building cross-platform mobile apps.

React Native has become one of the most popular frameworks for developing mobile applications due to its ability to allow developers to build apps using JavaScript and React. By enabling code reuse across both iOS and Android, React Native dramatically reduces development time and costs, making it a powerful choice for mobile app development. But like any powerful tool, React Native requires an understanding of its features, best practices, and the underlying concepts that make it work.

This book is structured to take you on a journey, from the basics to advanced topics, ensuring that you not only understand how to build apps with React Native but also how to leverage its features effectively. Whether you're building your first app or looking to enhance your existing knowledge, this book will guide you through each stage of the app development lifecycle. Here's what you can expect:

Starting with the Basics

The first sections of the book will introduce you to the fundamentals of React Native. You'll start by setting up your development environment and creating your first simple React Native app. Along the way, you'll gain a solid understanding of key concepts such as:

- **JSX (JavaScript XML)**: Learn how to write UI components using JSX, the syntax that blends JavaScript and HTML-like structures in React Native.
- **Components**: Understand the building blocks of a React Native app—functional and class components—and how to manage state and props to control the flow of data in your app.
- **Navigation**: Learn how to move users between screens with React Navigation, one of the most widely used navigation libraries in React Native.

Building Real-World Applications

Once you're familiar with the basics, this book takes you through the process of building real-world applications. You'll dive into more complex topics such as:

- **Firebase Integration**: Learn how to integrate Firebase for real-time messaging, authentication, and cloud data storage. This knowledge is vital for building apps that require backend support without the need for complex server-side infrastructure.

- **Push Notifications**: Discover how to implement push notifications to keep users engaged and informed, even when they're not actively using your app.

- **WebSockets**: Master WebSockets for real-time communication, a critical skill for apps like chat applications, live sports trackers, and any app that requires real-time data synchronization.

Optimizing Performance

With your apps taking shape, it's time to focus on performance. React Native apps, like any other mobile apps, require optimization to run smoothly across a variety of devices. In this book, you'll explore:

- **Performance Profiling**: Learn how to identify and eliminate performance bottlenecks using React Native's built-in profiling tools.

- **Memory Management**: Discover techniques for preventing memory leaks and managing memory effectively to ensure your app runs smoothly, even on devices with limited resources.

- **Rendering Optimization**: Learn how to optimize rendering performance by using tools like **React.memo** and **PureComponent**, which can help reduce unnecessary re-renders and speed up your app's UI.

Testing and Debugging

One of the most important aspects of any app development process is ensuring that your app works as expected. This book covers various testing techniques and debugging practices that will help you maintain a reliable and error-free app:

- **Unit Testing**: Learn how to test individual components and functions using **Jest**, the default testing framework for React Native.
- **UI Testing**: Discover how to automate UI testing with **Detox** and **Appium**, tools that allow you to simulate real user interactions and ensure that your app behaves as expected.
- **Debugging Tools**: Master debugging strategies using **Chrome Developer Tools, React Native Debugger**, and **Performance Monitors** to identify and resolve issues effectively.

Deploying and Managing Your App

After completing your app, you'll need to deploy it to the **App Store** and **Google Play**. This book guides you through the steps

9

of preparing your app for release, from configuring app icons and splash screens to meeting the platform-specific guidelines. You'll also learn:

- **Submitting to the App Store and Google Play**: Step-by-step instructions on how to upload your app, submit it for review, and handle app versioning and updates.
- **Handling App Updates**: Tips on how to manage app versions and release updates without interrupting the user experience.

Staying Up-to-Date with the React Native Ecosystem

The React Native ecosystem is constantly evolving. This book not only teaches you how to use React Native today but also provides strategies for staying up-to-date with the latest releases, tools, and best practices. You'll learn about:

- **Popular libraries** and **tools** that enhance your development workflow.
- **Community resources** like forums, newsletters, and podcasts that keep you connected to the ever-growing world of React Native.

Real-World Projects and Examples

Throughout the book, you will build practical, real-world projects that integrate everything you've learned:

10

- **Real-Time Chat App**: You will develop a messaging app using **Firebase** for real-time messaging and **push notifications** for user alerts.

- **To-Do List App with Notifications**: You'll build a to-do list app that allows users to set tasks, get notified about upcoming deadlines, and keep track of their progress.

- **Other Sample Projects**: The book also includes other practical app examples to help reinforce the concepts and give you a better understanding of how to apply them to real-world projects.

Who This Book Is For

This book is designed for:

- **Beginner developers** who are new to React Native and mobile app development.

- **Intermediate developers** who are familiar with JavaScript and React and want to dive into building mobile applications.

- **Experienced developers** looking to learn React Native, expand their skill set, or transition from native mobile development.

By the end of this book, you'll be equipped with the knowledge and experience to build your own cross-platform apps, optimize their performance, and navigate the entire app development lifecycle—from development to deployment.

Why React Native?

React Native has become a popular choice for mobile app development due to its flexibility and efficiency. By allowing developers to write code once in **JavaScript** and run it on both **iOS** and **Android**, React Native eliminates the need for separate development teams for different platforms, reducing both time and costs. React Native also provides a rich ecosystem of libraries, tools, and community support, making it an excellent choice for building high-quality, production-ready mobile applications.

Let's Begin!

In this book, you'll not only learn how to build React Native apps but also how to create beautiful, performant, and user-friendly mobile experiences. Let's dive in and start building your first React Native app!

CHAPTER 1

INTRODUCTION TO REACT NATIVE AND CROSS-PLATFORM DEVELOPMENT

Overview of Mobile App Development

Mobile app development has grown rapidly over the past decade, evolving from simple applications to sophisticated systems that power everything from daily tasks to complex business operations. Developers have the option to build apps for different platforms, primarily iOS and Android, the two dominant operating systems in the mobile market.

Traditionally, building mobile apps for iOS and Android involved using different programming languages and development environments. For iOS, developers used Swift (or Objective-C), and for Android, Java/Kotlin was the go-to language. This meant writing separate codebases for each platform, leading to longer development cycles and higher costs.

However, as mobile usage exploded, the need for faster and more efficient development processes grew. Cross-platform development emerged as a solution to create a single codebase that could run on multiple platforms, saving time, effort, and costs. React Native is one of the leading frameworks that enable this.

Introduction to Cross-Platform Development with React Native

Cross-platform development refers to the practice of writing a single codebase that can run on both iOS and Android, as opposed to developing separate apps for each platform. React Native, developed by Facebook, is one of the most popular frameworks for cross-platform mobile development.

React Native allows developers to use JavaScript and React, a popular JavaScript library for building user interfaces, to write mobile apps. It enables the reuse of most of the code across both platforms, which significantly reduces development time and costs. React Native uses native components, which means it doesn't compromise on performance or user experience.

Benefits of Using React Native for iOS and Android Apps

1. **Code Reusability**: The main advantage of React Native is that it allows developers to write a single codebase that works for both iOS and Android. This means significant savings in development time and costs, as developers don't need to write separate code for each platform.

2. **Faster Development**: React Native speeds up development due to its "hot-reloading" feature, which allows developers to instantly see changes in the app

without rebuilding it. This enhances productivity and streamlines the development cycle.

3. **Native Performance**: While React Native uses JavaScript, it can access native components and APIs. This ensures that apps built with React Native perform nearly as well as those written natively in Swift or Java/Kotlin.

4. **Large Community and Ecosystem**: React Native has a large and active community, which means developers have access to a wealth of resources, libraries, and tools. This community support makes it easier to find solutions to challenges and stay up to date with the latest best practices.

5. **Third-Party Plugin Support**: React Native allows the integration of third-party plugins, such as maps, payment gateways, and analytics tools, to enhance the functionality of your app without compromising performance.

6. **Cross-Platform Compatibility**: React Native enables code sharing not just between iOS and Android, but also between the web and mobile apps, allowing for a more consistent experience across all platforms.

How React Native Compares to Other Mobile Development Frameworks

React Native is not the only framework for cross-platform development. Other popular frameworks, such as Flutter,

Xamarin, and Ionic, also offer solutions for building mobile apps across multiple platforms. Here's how React Native compares to them:

1. **React Native vs. Flutter**:
   o **React Native** is based on JavaScript and React, making it a natural choice for developers already familiar with JavaScript. It provides near-native performance and uses native components for rendering.
   o **Flutter**, developed by Google, uses Dart as its programming language and offers an entirely custom rendering engine. Flutter can achieve superior performance in some cases but requires developers to learn Dart, which might be a barrier for some.

2. **React Native vs. Xamarin**:
   o **Xamarin** is based on C# and .NET, allowing developers to use their existing skills in C# to build cross-platform apps. While Xamarin provides a close-to-native experience, it can sometimes fall behind in terms of performance and community support compared to React Native.

3. **React Native vs. Ionic**:
   o **Ionic** uses web technologies like HTML, CSS, and JavaScript to create mobile apps. While it is

ideal for building hybrid apps that run in a webview, it generally doesn't offer the same performance as React Native, which uses native components. Ionic is more suited for simpler apps that don't require native-like performance.

In summary, React Native strikes a balance between performance and ease of use, offering a robust solution for developers who want to build high-performance apps with a unified codebase for both iOS and Android. While other frameworks have their own strengths, React Native's combination of performance, cross-platform compatibility, and developer experience makes it a leading choice for modern mobile app development.

CHAPTER 2

SETTING UP THE

DEVELOPMENT ENVIRONMENT

Installing Node.js and npm

Before you can start working with React Native, you'll need to set up the core development tools: **Node.js** and **npm** (Node Package Manager). These are essential for managing JavaScript packages and running React Native projects.

1. **Install Node.js**:
    - o   Visit the Node.js official website.
    - o   Download the recommended version for your operating system (either LTS or Current).
    - o   Run the installer and follow the prompts to complete the installation.
    - o   To verify the installation, open a terminal or command prompt and type:

    ```bash
    node -v
    ```

    This command will return the installed version of Node.js.

2. **Install npm**:

- o npm comes bundled with Node.js, so it will automatically be installed when you install Node.js.
- o You can verify that npm is installed by typing the following command in the terminal:

```bash
npm -v
```

This will return the version of npm installed on your system.

Setting Up React Native CLI or Expo CLI

React Native offers two main ways to start development: the **React Native CLI** and **Expo CLI**. Both have their advantages, and the choice depends on your project needs.

React Native CLI

React Native CLI gives you full control over your development environment, allowing you to configure and customize everything. This approach is ideal for more advanced use cases.

1. **Install React Native CLI**:

o Open your terminal and run the following command to install the React Native CLI globally:

```
bash


npm install -g react-native-cli
```

o Once the CLI is installed, you can create a new React Native project by running:

```
bash


npx react-native init MyNewApp
```

This will create a new project called `MyNewApp` in a directory of the same name.

Expo CLI

Expo is a more beginner-friendly option, providing a set of tools and services to make React Native development faster and easier. With Expo, you can get started quickly without needing to worry about native dependencies or configuring Android Studio and Xcode right away.

1. **Install Expo CLI**:
   o To install Expo CLI, run the following command in your terminal:

20

```
bash
```

```
npm install -g expo-cli
```

o You can then create a new Expo project by running:

```
bash
```

```
expo init MyNewApp
```

You'll be prompted to choose a template (blank, tabs, or a more advanced option). After you make your choice, Expo will set up the project.

2. **Running an Expo project**:
   o Once your project is created, navigate into the project folder:

```
bash
```

```
cd MyNewApp
```

   o Start the development server:

```
bash
```

```
expo start
```

o This will open the Expo Developer Tools in your browser, and you'll be able to run the app on your mobile device or simulator using the Expo Go app.

Setting Up Android Studio and Xcode

To run React Native apps on Android and iOS, you need to set up Android Studio and Xcode for the respective platforms.

Setting Up Android Studio

1. **Download and Install Android Studio**:
   o Visit the Android Studio website.
   o Download the appropriate version for your operating system and follow the installation instructions.
   o After installation, launch Android Studio and ensure the Android SDK is set up correctly.
   o Install necessary dependencies, including the Android Emulator, which allows you to run your app on a virtual Android device.
2. **Setting Up Android Virtual Device (AVD)**:
   o Open Android Studio and go to **Tools** > **AVD Manager**.
   o Click **Create Virtual Device**, choose a device model (e.g., Pixel), and select a system image

(choose one based on the Android version you want to test).

o Follow the prompts to create the virtual device, then start it to emulate an Android device.

Setting Up Xcode (for macOS only)

1. **Download and Install Xcode**:
   o Xcode is only available on macOS, and it's required for building iOS apps. Download Xcode from the Mac App Store.
   o After installation, open Xcode and ensure that the Xcode Command Line Tools are installed. Go to **Xcode > Preferences > Locations** and check if the Command Line Tools are selected.

2. **Install CocoaPods**:
   o CocoaPods is a dependency manager for iOS, and it's used to manage the libraries your app depends on. To install CocoaPods, run the following command:

```bash

sudo gem install cocoapods
```

   o After installing CocoaPods, navigate to your project directory and run:

```
bash

cd ios
pod install
```

This ensures all necessary iOS dependencies are installed.

Running Your First "Hello World" App

Now that your development environment is set up, let's create and run a simple "Hello World" app.

Using React Native CLI:

1. Open your terminal, navigate to the folder where you want your project, and run:

```
bash

npx react-native init HelloWorldApp
```

2. Navigate into your project directory:

```
bash

cd HelloWorldApp
```

3. Run the app on Android or iOS:
   o For Android:

```
bash
```

```
npx react-native run-android
```

- o For iOS (macOS only):

```
bash
```

```
npx react-native run-ios
```

Using Expo CLI:

1. Create a new Expo project by running:

```
bash
```

```
expo init HelloWorldApp
```

Choose a blank template when prompted.

2. Navigate to the project directory:

```
bash
```

```
cd HelloWorldApp
```

3. Start the development server:

```
bash
```

```
expo start
```

4. Scan the QR code with the **Expo Go** app on your mobile device to see the app running.

The "Hello World" app will display a simple greeting, confirming that your development environment is correctly set up. You're now ready to start building your mobile apps with React Native!

CHAPTER 3

UNDERSTANDING REACT BASICS

Overview of React Concepts

React is a popular JavaScript library used to build user interfaces, particularly for single-page applications. It was developed by Facebook and has become the go-to tool for building dynamic web and mobile applications. Below are the key concepts that form the foundation of React development:

1. **JSX (JavaScript XML)**:
   - **JSX** is a syntax extension for JavaScript that allows you to write HTML elements in your JavaScript code. It looks similar to HTML but is actually a syntax sugar for React's `React.createElement()` method.
   - JSX makes it easier to create UI components because it allows you to write markup directly in JavaScript.
   - Example:

   ```javascript
   ```

```
const    element    =    <h1>Hello,
world!</h1>;
```

- o In the above example, the <h1> element is JSX, which React will render as a DOM element when the component is loaded.

2. **Components**:

- o **Components** are the building blocks of React applications. A component is essentially a JavaScript function or class that returns JSX and manages how the UI should look based on data (state and props).
- o Components allow you to split the UI into independent, reusable pieces, making your code more modular and easier to manage.
- o There are two types of components: **Functional Components** and **Class Components** (explained below).

3. **State**:

- o **State** is a fundamental concept in React used to manage data that changes over time in a component. When the state of a component changes, React re-renders that component to reflect the new data.
- o Example of setting state in a functional component:

28

```javascript

const    [count,    setCount]    =
useState(0);
```

In this example, `count` is the state variable, and `setCount` is the function used to update that state. The component will re-render whenever `count` changes.

4. **Props (Properties)**:
   o **Props** are used to pass data from a parent component to a child component. They are immutable, meaning that a child component cannot modify the props it receives; it can only read them.
   o Props allow components to be reusable by passing different data to them from different parts of the application.
   o Example:

```javascript

function Greeting(props) {
   return              <h1>Hello,
{props.name}!</h1>;
}
```

```
<Greeting name="John" />
```

In this case, `name` is passed as a prop from the parent component to the `Greeting` component.

Functional Components vs. Class Components

React allows you to build components using either **functional components** or **class components**. Both types of components achieve the same goal, but there are some important differences.

1. **Functional Components**:
   - Functional components are JavaScript functions that take in `props` as arguments and return JSX.
   - They are simpler, easier to read, and were the preferred way to write React components before the introduction of hooks.
   - With the introduction of **React hooks**, functional components can now also manage state and side effects, making them more powerful.
   - Example:

   ```javascript
   function MyComponent(props) {
     return <div>{props.message}</div>;
   }
   ```

2. **Class Components**:

   o Class components are ES6 classes that extend the `React.Component` class. They can hold and manage internal state, and they have access to lifecycle methods (discussed below).

   o Class components were the primary way to manage state and side effects before hooks were introduced.

   o Example:

```javascript
class MyComponent extends
React.Component {
  render() {
    return
<div>{this.props.message}</div>;
  }
}
```

Differences:

- Functional components are generally preferred for their simplicity and ease of use.
- Class components are still useful for understanding legacy React code, but most modern React codebases use functional components with hooks.

31

React Lifecycle Methods

Lifecycle methods are special functions in class components that allow you to hook into different phases of a component's life cycle. In functional components, similar functionality is achieved using **hooks** such as `useEffect`.

Here's an overview of the lifecycle methods available in class components:

1. **Mounting (When a component is created and added to the DOM):**
   - `constructor()`: This is the first method that gets called when an instance of the component is created. It is used to initialize state and bind methods.
   - `componentDidMount()`: This method is called once the component has been rendered to the screen. It's useful for loading data from an API or performing any setup that requires access to the DOM.

   javascript

   ```javascript
   componentDidMount() {
     console.log("Component        has
   mounted.");
   }
   ```

2. **Updating (When a component's state or props change)**:

   o `shouldComponentUpdate()`: This method allows you to control when a component should update based on changes in state or props. It's a performance optimization method that helps avoid unnecessary re-renders.

   o `componentDidUpdate()`: This method is called after the component has re-rendered due to changes in state or props. It's useful for performing actions after the update, such as making network requests or updating other parts of the UI.

   ```javascript
   componentDidUpdate(prevProps, prevState) {
       if      (this.state.count      !==
   prevState.count) {
           console.log("Count         has
   changed");
       }
   }
   ```

3. **Unmounting (When a component is removed from the DOM)**:

o componentWillUnmount(): This method is called right before a component is removed from the DOM. It's typically used for cleanup tasks, such as clearing timers or canceling network requests.

```javascript
componentWillUnmount() {
    console.log("Component    is    being
removed from the DOM.");
}
```

In **functional components**, lifecycle behavior is handled with the useEffect hook, which can serve a similar purpose. For example, to mimic componentDidMount and componentDidUpdate, you can use useEffect like this:

```javascript
useEffect(() => {
   console.log("Component mounted or updated");
}, [state]); // The effect runs whenever 'state'
changes.
```

The useEffect hook can replace most lifecycle methods and is a key feature for functional components, making them more powerful and capable of managing side effects like data fetching, subscriptions, and timers.

Summary

In this chapter, we introduced key React concepts like JSX, components, state, and props. We compared functional and class components, highlighting how functional components are the modern approach to building React apps with the help of hooks. Finally, we explored lifecycle methods in class components and the `useEffect` hook in functional components, both of which allow developers to control the behavior of their app at different stages of a component's life cycle. Understanding these basics is essential for building effective, efficient React Native apps.

CHAPTER 4

CREATING YOUR FIRST REACT NATIVE APP

Setting Up a New Project

Now that you've set up your development environment, it's time to create your first React Native app. There are two primary ways to start a new React Native project: using the **React Native CLI** or **Expo CLI**. In this chapter, we'll focus on using the React Native CLI, which is ideal for developers who want full control over the native code.

1. **Creating a React Native Project with React Native CLI:**

   o First, open your terminal and run the following command to create a new React Native project:

   ```bash

   npx react-native init FirstApp
   ```

   This command initializes a new project named `FirstApp` in a folder with the same name.

o Once the project is created, navigate into the project directory:

```bash

cd FirstApp
```

2. **Creating a React Native Project with Expo CLI**:

o If you're using Expo CLI, which is ideal for quick development without worrying about native code, run:

```bash

expo init FirstApp
```

o After selecting a template (you can choose the "blank" template), navigate into the project folder:

```bash

cd FirstApp
```

o Expo provides a simpler setup, but it does have some limitations when dealing with native code, which we will cover later.

Writing the First React Native Component

Once your project is set up, it's time to write your first component. React Native uses **JavaScript** and **JSX** to define components, which you can later render to the screen.

1. **Open the App.js file**: In your project directory, open the App.js file. This file is the main entry point of your app.
2. **Write a Basic Component**: Replace the default content in App.js with the following code to create a simple "Hello World" app:

```javascript
import React from 'react';
import { View, Text, StyleSheet } from 'react-native';

const App = () => {
  return (
    <View style={styles.container}>
      <Text style={styles.text}>Hello, React Native!</Text>
    </View>
  );
};

const styles = StyleSheet.create({
  container: {
```

```
    flex: 1,
    justifyContent: 'center',
    alignItems: 'center',
    backgroundColor: '#fff',
  },
  text: {
    fontSize: 20,
    fontWeight: 'bold',
  },
});

export default App;
```

- o **Explanation**:
  - `View`: A basic component used to wrap other elements.
  - `Text`: Displays text on the screen.
  - `StyleSheet.create()`: A method to define styles in a consistent way.
  - The `App` component returns JSX, which React Native interprets to display the UI.

Running the App on Android and iOS Simulators

To see your app in action, you need to run it on a simulator or a real device. React Native supports both Android and iOS simulators. Here's how to run your app on both:

1. **Running on Android Simulator**:

39

o First, make sure you have Android Studio and an Android Emulator set up (as described in Chapter 2).

o Open your terminal, navigate to the project folder, and run:

```bash

npx react-native run-android
```

o This command will compile the app and launch it on the Android Emulator. If you have a physical Android device connected via USB, it will run on that device instead.

2. **Running on iOS Simulator (macOS only)**:

o For macOS users, you can run your app on the iOS simulator. First, make sure you have Xcode installed (as discussed in Chapter 2).

o Open your terminal, navigate to the project folder, and run:

```bash

npx react-native run-ios
```

o This command will compile the app and launch it on the default iOS Simulator. If you want to specify a particular device, use:

```
bash

npx     react-native     run-ios     --
simulator="iPhone 12"
```

o   If you're using Expo CLI, you can also run the app on a physical device by scanning the QR code displayed in the Expo Developer Tools with the Expo Go app.

Debugging Basics

During development, you'll encounter issues and bugs that need to be fixed. React Native provides several tools to help you with debugging.

1. **Using the Developer Menu**:
    o   On both Android and iOS, you can open the developer menu to access useful debugging tools.
    o   On Android, shake your device or press `Cmd + M` (macOS) or `Ctrl + M` (Windows/Linux) in the emulator.
    o   On iOS, press `Cmd + D` in the iOS simulator.
    o   The developer menu includes options such as:
        ▪   **Reload**: Refresh the app.
        ▪   **Enable/Disable Fast Refresh**: Automatically reload components as you change the code.

41

- **Debug JS Remotely**: Open Chrome DevTools to debug JavaScript code.
- **Enable Live Reload**: Automatically reload the app when you save changes to your code.

2. **Using Console Logs**:

   o You can add `console.log()` statements in your code to output values and debug logic. For example:

   ```javascript

   console.log('Hello     from     React Native');
   ```

   o These logs will appear in the console of your terminal or the browser console if you enable remote debugging.

3. **Debugging with Chrome Developer Tools**:

   o If you choose to debug remotely, you can open the Chrome Developer Tools by selecting "Debug JS Remotely" from the developer menu. This opens a new tab in Chrome, where you can inspect JavaScript errors, view console logs, and use breakpoints to step through your code.

4. **React Developer Tools**:

o The React Developer Tools extension (available for Chrome and Firefox) can be used to inspect the React component hierarchy and props/state in your app. This is particularly useful for inspecting the structure of your components and understanding how state and props change.

5. **Error Handling**:

o React Native will often provide helpful error messages directly in the app if something goes wrong. If an error occurs, a red screen (Red Screen of Death) will appear with an error message. You can use this message to identify the problem and fix it.

o It's a good practice to wrap your app's components in error boundaries to catch errors gracefully and avoid crashing the entire app.

Conclusion

In this chapter, you've learned how to:

- Set up a new React Native project using the React Native CLI.
- Write your first React Native component using JSX and display text on the screen.
- Run your app on both Android and iOS simulators to see your changes in real time.

- Use basic debugging tools, such as the developer menu and Chrome DevTools, to troubleshoot and fix issues in your app.

With your first app up and running, you're now ready to dive deeper into more complex features and functionality in React Native!

CHAPTER 5

CORE COMPONENTS OF REACT NATIVE

In this chapter, we will explore the core components of React Native, which are essential for creating mobile user interfaces. These components form the building blocks of your app and help structure the content and layout.

Text, View, Image, and ScrollView Components

React Native provides several core components for building user interfaces. Let's explore some of the most commonly used ones:

1. **Text**:
   - The Text component is used to display text on the screen. It supports various styles, such as font size, weight, and alignment, which allow you to customize how text looks.
   - Example:

   ```javascript

   import React from 'react';
   import { Text } from 'react-native';
   ```

```
const App = () => {
  return (
    <Text  style={{  fontSize:  20,
color:  'blue'  }}>Hello,  React
Native!</Text>
  );
};
export default App;
```

o The `Text` component also supports nesting, meaning you can include multiple pieces of text with different styles within a single `Text` element.

2. **View**:

o The `View` component is the most common container in React Native. It's used to wrap other components and apply styles like padding, margins, borders, and backgrounds. It functions similarly to a `div` in web development.

o Example:

```
javascript

import React from 'react';
import { View, Text } from 'react-
native';

const App = () => {
```

```
return (
    <View    style={{    flex:    1,
justifyContent:             'center',
alignItems: 'center' }}>
        <Text>Hello   from   a   View
component!</Text>
    </View>
  );
};
export default App;
```

- o View can be nested to create more complex layouts, and it supports flexbox for alignment and distribution.

3. **Image**:

   - o The Image component allows you to display images in your app. It supports both local images (stored in your project) and remote images (hosted on the web).
   - o Example (local image):

```javascript

import React from 'react';
import { Image } from 'react-native';

const App = () => {
  return (
    <Image
```

47

```
source={require('./assets/logo.png'
)}
      style={{ width: 200, height:
200 }}
    />
  );
};
export default App;
```

o   Example (remote image):

```javascript
import React from 'react';
import { Image } from 'react-native';

const App = () => {
  return (
    <Image
      source={{                uri:
'https://example.com/image.jpg' }}
      style={{ width: 200, height:
200 }}
    />
  );
};
export default App;
```

4. **ScrollView**:

o The `ScrollView` component is used when you need a scrollable container. It allows content to be scrolled vertically or horizontally. It's especially useful when the content inside the container exceeds the screen size.

o Example:

```javascript
import React from 'react';
import { ScrollView, Text } from 'react-native';

const App = () => {
  return (
    <ScrollView>
      <Text style={{ fontSize: 18 }}>Item 1</Text>
      <Text style={{ fontSize: 18 }}>Item 2</Text>
      <Text style={{ fontSize: 18 }}>Item 3</Text>
      {/* Add more items to make the content scrollable */}
    </ScrollView>
  );
};
export default App;
```

Working with Basic Layouts and Styles

React Native uses a flexible layout system that is largely based on **Flexbox**, a layout model originally designed for the web. Flexbox enables you to arrange components in a row or column and align them easily.

1. **Basic Layouts with Flexbox**:
   - The basic principle of Flexbox is that it works by applying properties like `flexDirection`, `justifyContent`, and `alignItems` to arrange elements.
   - `flexDirection`: Defines the direction of the main axis. It can either be `row` (horizontal) or `column` (vertical).
   - `justifyContent`: Aligns children components along the main axis.
   - `alignItems`: Aligns children components along the cross axis (perpendicular to the main axis).

   Example:

   ```javascript
   import React from 'react';
   import { View, Text } from 'react-native';

   const App = () => {
   ```

```
  return (
    <View style={{ flex: 1, flexDirection:
'row', justifyContent: 'space-around' }}>
      <Text    style={{    backgroundColor:
'skyblue', padding: 10 }}>Item 1</Text>
      <Text    style={{    backgroundColor:
'salmon', padding: 10 }}>Item 2</Text>
      <Text    style={{    backgroundColor:
'lightgreen', padding: 10 }}>Item 3</Text>
    </View>
  );
};
export default App;
```

- In this example, `flexDirection: 'row'` arranges the items horizontally, and `justifyContent: 'space-around'` ensures equal spacing between them.

2. **Aligning Items with Flexbox**:
   - **justifyContent**: This property aligns the components along the main axis.
     - Options include `flex-start`, `center`, `flex-end`, `space-between`, and `space-around`.
   - **alignItems**: This property aligns the components along the cross axis.
     - Options include `flex-start`, `center`, `flex-end`, `stretch`.

51

o **flex**: This property defines how much space a component should take up in a flex container. It is used to create flexible layouts.

Example of a vertically centered layout:

javascript

```
import React from 'react';
import { View, Text } from 'react-native';

const App = () => {
  return (
    <View style={{ flex: 1,
justifyContent: 'center', alignItems:
'center' }}>
      <Text>Hello, React Native!</Text>
    </View>
  );
};
export default App;
```

o In this example, justifyContent: 'center' aligns the text vertically, and alignItems: 'center' aligns it horizontally.

Using Flexbox for Layout Design

Flexbox is extremely useful in React Native for designing responsive layouts, especially when dealing with varying screen sizes across mobile devices.

1. **Creating a Simple Column Layout**:
   o To create a simple column layout, use `flexDirection: 'column'` (this is the default value for `flexDirection`).
   o Example:

   ```javascript
   import React from 'react';
   import { View, Text } from 'react-native';

   const App = () => {
     return (
       <View style={{ flex: 1,
   flexDirection: 'column',
   justifyContent: 'center' }}>
         <Text style={{
   backgroundColor: 'lightblue',
   padding: 10 }}>Item 1</Text>
         <Text style={{
   backgroundColor: 'lightcoral',
   padding: 10 }}>Item 2</Text>
   ```

```
      <Text                    style={{
  backgroundColor:       'lightgreen',
  padding: 10 }}>Item 3</Text>
    </View>
  );
};
export default App;
```

o   Here, the items will be stacked vertically, and
    `justifyContent: 'center'` ensures they are
    centered vertically within the container.

2. **Creating a Responsive Layout with Flexbox**:

o   React Native's Flexbox system makes it easy to
    create layouts that adjust dynamically to the
    screen size. You can use the `flex` property to
    define how much space a component should
    occupy in relation to its siblings.

Example (responsive layout with flexible items):

```javascript
import React from 'react';
import { View, Text } from 'react-native';

const App = () => {
  return (
    <View style={{ flex: 1, flexDirection:
'row' }}>
```

```
        <Text      style={{      flex:      1,
backgroundColor:  'skyblue',  padding:  10
}}>Item 1</Text>
        <Text      style={{      flex:      2,
backgroundColor:  'salmon',  padding:  10
}}>Item 2</Text>
        <Text      style={{      flex:      1,
backgroundColor: 'lightgreen', padding: 10
}}>Item 3</Text>
    </View>
  );
};
export default App;
```

o   In this layout, `Item 2` will take twice the space
    compared to `Item 1` and `Item 3`, making the
    layout flexible and responsive to different screen
    sizes.

Conclusion

In this chapter, we explored the core components of React Native:
`Text`, `View`, `Image`, and `ScrollView`. These components allow
you to create the basic structure and design of your app. We also
looked at how to use **Flexbox** for layout design, which is an
essential tool in React Native for creating responsive and flexible
layouts. By mastering these components and layout techniques,

you can create well-structured and visually appealing mobile applications.

CHAPTER 6

NAVIGATION IN REACT NATIVE

Navigating between different screens and sections of your mobile app is a crucial part of creating a seamless user experience. In React Native, the **React Navigation** library provides a flexible and customizable solution for managing navigation between screens.

Introduction to React Navigation Library

React Navigation is the most widely used navigation library for React Native applications. It provides an easy way to implement common navigation patterns like stack, tab, and drawer navigation. React Navigation supports both **Android** and **iOS**, and its declarative API makes it easy to set up and use.

To get started with React Navigation, you first need to install the library and its dependencies.

1. **Installing React Navigation**: Open your terminal and navigate to your project directory. Install the required packages by running:

   bash

```
npm install @react-navigation/native
```

In addition to the core navigation package, you'll need to install the following dependencies:

```
bash
```

```
npm install react-native-screens react-native-safe-area-context
```

For handling stack navigation, you also need to install the stack navigator:

```
bash
```

```
npm install @react-navigation/stack
```

If you are planning to use tab or drawer navigation, install the respective packages:

```
bash
```

```
npm install @react-navigation/bottom-tabs
npm install @react-navigation/drawer
```

2. **Setting Up Navigation Container**: React Navigation requires a **NavigationContainer** to manage the navigation state of your app. The container must wrap your app's navigation structure.

Example of setting up the container in `App.js`:

```javascript
import * as React from 'react';
import { NavigationContainer } from '@react-navigation/native';
import { createStackNavigator } from '@react-navigation/stack';
import HomeScreen from './screens/HomeScreen';
import DetailsScreen from './screens/DetailsScreen';

const Stack = createStackNavigator();

function App() {
  return (
    <NavigationContainer>
      <Stack.Navigator initialRouteName="Home">
        <Stack.Screen name="Home" component={HomeScreen} />
        <Stack.Screen name="Details" component={DetailsScreen} />
      </Stack.Navigator>
    </NavigationContainer>
  );
}
```

```
export default App;
```

In the example above, **NavigationContainer** wraps the entire navigation structure, and **Stack.Navigator** is used to set up stack navigation between two screens: HomeScreen and DetailsScreen.

Stack, Tab, and Drawer Navigation

React Navigation provides different types of navigators to implement various navigation patterns. The three most commonly used navigators are **Stack Navigator**, **Tab Navigator**, and **Drawer Navigator**.

1. Stack Navigation:

Stack navigation allows users to navigate through a stack of screens, where each new screen is pushed on top of the stack and can be popped off to return to the previous screen.

- **Creating a Stack Navigator**: The example above demonstrates a basic stack navigator with HomeScreen and DetailsScreen. When the user navigates from HomeScreen to DetailsScreen, DetailsScreen is pushed onto the stack.
- **Navigation Actions**: To navigate between screens, you can use the navigation prop. Example:

```javascript

function HomeScreen({ navigation }) {
  return (
    <View>
      <Button
        title="Go to Details"
        onPress={()                          =>
navigation.navigate('Details')}
      />
    </View>
  );
}
```

In this example, `navigation.navigate('Details')` will push the `DetailsScreen` onto the stack when the button is pressed.

2. Tab Navigation:

Tab navigation provides a navigation bar at the bottom of the screen, with each tab linking to a different screen. This is typically used for apps that have a fixed set of views that are accessed directly from the bottom navigation bar.

- **Creating a Tab Navigator**: Install the tab navigator library:

```bash
```

```
npm install @react-navigation/bottom-tabs
```

Then, define a tab navigator in your `App.js`:

```javascript

import * as React from 'react';
import { NavigationContainer } from
'@react-navigation/native';
import { createBottomTabNavigator } from
'@react-navigation/bottom-tabs';
import HomeScreen from
'./screens/HomeScreen';
import SettingsScreen from
'./screens/SettingsScreen';

const Tab = createBottomTabNavigator();

function App() {
  return (
    <NavigationContainer>
      <Tab.Navigator>
        <Tab.Screen name="Home"
component={HomeScreen} />
        <Tab.Screen name="Settings"
component={SettingsScreen} />
      </Tab.Navigator>
    </NavigationContainer>
  );
```

```
}
```

```
export default App;
```

In this example, `HomeScreen` and `SettingsScreen` are two tabs that users can navigate between.

3. Drawer Navigation:

Drawer navigation provides a sliding panel (drawer) that typically contains a list of links or navigation options. It's ideal for apps with many sections or features that should be easily accessible.

- **Creating a Drawer Navigator**: Install the drawer navigator library:

bash

```
npm install @react-navigation/drawer
```

Then, define a drawer navigator in your `App.js`:

javascript

```
import * as React from 'react';
import { NavigationContainer } from
'@react-navigation/native';
import { createDrawerNavigator } from
'@react-navigation/drawer';
```

```
import              HomeScreen              from
'./screens/HomeScreen';
import            ProfileScreen             from
'./screens/ProfileScreen';

const Drawer = createDrawerNavigator();

function App() {
  return (
    <NavigationContainer>
      <Drawer.Navigator>
        <Drawer.Screen           name="Home"
component={HomeScreen} />
        <Drawer.Screen         name="Profile"
component={ProfileScreen} />
      </Drawer.Navigator>
    </NavigationContainer>
  );
}

export default App;
```

In this example, the app features a drawer that users can slide in to access HomeScreen and ProfileScreen.

Handling Navigation Between Screens

React Navigation uses the **navigation prop** to handle navigation between screens. You can use various methods like `navigate()`, `push()`, `goBack()`, and `reset()` to manage screen transitions.

1. **Navigate**: Navigate to a different screen.

   javascript

   ```javascript
   navigation.navigate('ScreenName');
   ```

2. **Push**: Push a new screen onto the stack, even if it's already in the stack.

   javascript

   ```javascript
   navigation.push('ScreenName');
   ```

3. **Go Back**: Go back to the previous screen.

   javascript

   ```javascript
   navigation.goBack();
   ```

4. **Reset**: Reset the navigation state and navigate to a new screen, clearing the stack.

   javascript

```
navigation.reset({
  index: 0,
  routes: [{ name: 'Home' }],
});
```

Customizing Navigation

React Navigation allows you to customize your navigators to suit your app's design and functionality. You can add icons, modify screen titles, and apply custom styling to navigators and screens.

For example, to add icons to a tab navigator, you can use libraries like **React Native Vector Icons**:

bash

```
npm install react-native-vector-icons
```

Then, use icons in the tab navigator like so:

javascript

```
import { Ionicons } from '@react-native-vector-icons/Ionicons';

<Tab.Screen
  name="Home"
  component={HomeScreen}
  options={{
    tabBarIcon: ({ color, size }) => (
```

```
        <Ionicons     name="home"     color={color}
size={size} />
    ),
  }}
/>
```

Conclusion

In this chapter, we introduced the **React Navigation** library and explored how to use **Stack**, **Tab**, and **Drawer navigators** to manage navigation between different screens in your React Native app. You also learned how to handle navigation actions using the `navigation` prop and customize the navigators for a better user experience. By mastering navigation in React Native, you can create fluid, seamless, and intuitive mobile applications that are easy to navigate.

CHAPTER 7

MANAGING STATE AND PROPS IN REACT NATIVE

In this chapter, we will dive into two fundamental concepts in React Native: **state** and **props**. Understanding how to manage and pass data within your application is essential for creating dynamic and interactive mobile apps. We'll also explore how the **useState** and **useEffect** hooks simplify state management and component lifecycle in functional components.

State vs Props in React

1. **State**:
    - **State** refers to the data that is specific to a component and can change over time. Each component can maintain its own state, and when the state of a component changes, React will re-render that component to reflect the new state.
    - State is mutable (can be changed), and it's used when you need to track user inputs, form values, toggles, or any other data that can change over time.
    - Example:

```javascript
import React, { useState } from
'react';
import { View, Text, Button } from
'react-native';

const Counter = () => {
  const [count, setCount] =
useState(0);   // Declaring state
variable 'count'

  return (
    <View>
      <Text>Count: {count}</Text>
      <Button      title="Increment"
onPress={() => setCount(count + 1)}
/>
    </View>
  );
};

export default Counter;
```

o   In this example, the count variable is part of the component's state, and the setCount function updates it. Each time the button is pressed, the state is updated, and the component re-renders to reflect the new count.

69

2. **Props (Properties)**:

- o **Props** are read-only values that are passed to a component from its parent. Unlike state, props cannot be changed directly within the component that receives them. They are immutable and provide a way to pass data and event handlers from one component to another.

- o Props are commonly used to pass data from parent components to child components, making components reusable with different inputs.

- o Example:

```javascript
import React from 'react';
import { View, Text } from 'react-native';

const Greeting = (props) => {
  return                <Text>Hello,
{props.name}!</Text>;
};

const App = () => {
  return (
    <View>
      <Greeting name="Alice" />
      <Greeting name="Bob" />
```

70

```
      </View>
    );
};
```

```
export default App;
```

- o In this example, the `Greeting` component receives the `name` prop from the `App` component, which allows it to render personalized greetings. Props are passed down from the parent (`App`) to the child (`Greeting`), and each `Greeting` component gets a different name.

Using `useState` and `useEffect` Hooks

React's functional components have hooks like `useState` and `useEffect` to manage state and handle side effects (such as fetching data or updating the DOM).

1. **useState**:
   - o The `useState` hook allows you to add state to functional components. It returns an array with two elements: the current state value and a function to update that value.
   - o Syntax:

   ```
   javascript
   ```

```
const      [state,      setState]      =
useState(initialValue);
```

- state: The current value of the state variable.
- setState: A function used to update the state.

Example:

```
javascript

import React, { useState } from 'react';
import { View, Text, Button } from 'react-native';

const Toggle = () => {
  const    [isToggled,    setIsToggled]    =
useState(false);   // Declare state

  const toggleSwitch = () => {
    setIsToggled(!isToggled);    // Update
state
  };

  return (
    <View>
      <Text>{isToggled ? 'Switch is ON' :
'Switch is OFF'}</Text>
```

```
      <Button               title="Toggle"
onPress={toggleSwitch} />
    </View>
  );
};


export default Toggle;
```

- o In this example, the state isToggled tracks whether the switch is on or off, and the toggleSwitch function updates this state when the button is pressed.

2. **useEffect**:

- o The useEffect hook allows you to perform side effects in your functional components. A side effect could be something like fetching data from an API, subscribing to a data stream, or manually changing the DOM.
- o The useEffect hook runs after every render of the component, unless you specify dependencies (using the second argument) to limit when the effect should run.
- o Syntax:

```
javascript

useEffect(() => {
    // Code to run on every render
```

```
}, [dependencies]); // Optional:
only run when dependencies change
```

o **Example (fetching data):**

```javascript
import React, { useState, useEffect
} from 'react';
import { View, Text } from 'react-
native';

const DataFetcher = () => {
  const [data, setData] =
useState(null);

  useEffect(() => {

fetch('https://api.example.com/data
')
      .then(response =>
response.json())
      .then(json => setData(json));
  }, []); // Empty dependency array:
runs only once when component mounts

  return (
    <View>
```

```
    <Text>{data                    ?
JSON.stringify(data)              :
'Loading...'}</Text>
    </View>
  );
};
```

```
export default DataFetcher;
```

o In this example, `useEffect` runs once when the component mounts and fetches data from an API. The empty dependency array (`[]`) ensures that the effect runs only once, similar to `componentDidMount()` in class components.

o **Effect Cleanup**: If your effect returns a function, that function will be used to clean up when the component unmounts or before the effect runs again. This is useful for cleaning up subscriptions or timers.

```
javascript
```

```javascript
useEffect(() => {
  const interval = setInterval(() =>
{
    console.log('Interval running');
  }, 1000);

  // Cleanup function
```

```
return            ()                =>
clearInterval(interval);
}, []);    // Runs once on mount,
cleans up on unmount
```

Passing Data Between Components Using Props

Props provide a way to pass data between components. They allow you to share data from a parent component to a child component.

1. **Passing Props Down from Parent to Child**:
   - o In React, the parent component can pass props to its children. The child component receives props as an argument and uses them to render content.
   - o Example:

```javascript
import React from 'react';
import { View, Text } from 'react-native';

const Child = ({ message }) => {
  return <Text>{message}</Text>;
};

const Parent = () => {
  const parentMessage = 'Hello from Parent!';
```

```
return (
  <View>
    <Child message={parentMessage}
/>
  </View>
  );
};
```

```
export default Parent;
```

- o In this example, `Parent` passes a `message` prop to `Child`, which then renders it. This makes the `Child` component reusable with different values for the `message` prop.

2. **Passing Data Between Multiple Components**:
   - o Props can also be passed down through several layers of components. You can chain props from one component to another until they reach the component that needs them.
   - o Example:

```
javascript
```

```
import React from 'react';
import { View, Text } from 'react-
native';
```

```
const Grandchild = ({ message }) =>
{
```

77

```
    return <Text>{message}</Text>;
};

const Child = ({ message }) => {
    return              <Grandchild
message={message} />;
};

const Parent = () => {
    const parentMessage = 'Hello from
Parent!';

    return (
      <View>
        <Child message={parentMessage}
/>
      </View>
    );
};

export default Parent;
```

o Here, `Parent` passes the `message` prop to `Child`, which then passes it to `Grandchild`, where the message is displayed.

Conclusion

In this chapter, we explored the crucial concepts of **state** and **props** in React Native. We discussed how **state** is mutable and used to track data that changes over time, while **props** are immutable and used to pass data between components. We also learned how to use the **useState** and **useEffect** hooks to manage state and handle side effects in functional components. Finally, we covered how to pass data between components using props, making components more dynamic and reusable.

By mastering these concepts, you'll be able to build interactive and data-driven applications that are easy to maintain and scale.

CHAPTER 8

WORKING WITH FORMS AND USER INPUT

Handling user input is a fundamental part of any mobile app. In this chapter, we will explore how to create forms, manage user input, and validate data in React Native. These are essential skills for building interactive apps that require user interaction, such as login forms, surveys, and settings pages.

Creating Text Inputs and Forms

React Native provides the **TextInput** component, which allows users to input text into your app. This component can be used for creating text fields, such as for entering a name, email address, or password. You can also combine multiple **TextInput** components to create full forms.

1. **Creating a Basic Text Input**: The **TextInput** component is used to collect input from users. You can set various properties to customize the appearance and behavior of the text field.

    Example:

```javascript

import React, { useState } from 'react';
import { View, TextInput, Text, StyleSheet } from 'react-native';

const App = () => {
  const [text, setText] = useState('');  // Managing the input state

  return (
    <View style={styles.container}>
      <TextInput
        style={styles.input}
        placeholder="Enter some text"
        value={text}   // Bind the input value to the state
        onChangeText={(newText)           => setText(newText)}  // Update state when the text changes
      />
      <Text>You typed: {text}</Text>
    </View>
  );
};

const styles = StyleSheet.create({
  container: {
    flex: 1,
```

```
    justifyContent: 'center',
    alignItems: 'center',
  },
  input: {
    height: 40,
    borderColor: 'gray',
    borderWidth: 1,
    marginBottom: 20,
    width: '80%',
    paddingHorizontal: 10,
  },
});
```

```
export default App;
```

In this example, the TextInput component is used to allow the user to type some text. The text is controlled by the useState hook, meaning that the value of the TextInput is bound to the component's state, and any changes made by the user are reflected in the state variable text.

2. **Creating a Form with Multiple Inputs**: Forms often involve multiple inputs, such as a name, email, and password. You can use multiple TextInput components and manage their values independently or together in the state.

Example (Form with name and email fields):

javascript

```
import React, { useState } from 'react';
import { View, TextInput, Button, Text,
StyleSheet } from 'react-native';

const App = () => {
  const [name, setName] = useState('');
  const [email, setEmail] = useState('');

  const handleSubmit = () => {
    console.log('Form Submitted');
    console.log('Name:', name);
    console.log('Email:', email);
  };

  return (
    <View style={styles.container}>
      <TextInput
        style={styles.input}
        placeholder="Enter your name"
        value={name}
        onChangeText={(text)              =>
setName(text)}
      />
      <TextInput
        style={styles.input}
        placeholder="Enter your email"
```

```
        value={email}
        onChangeText={(text)              =>
setEmail(text)}
      />
      <Button               title="Submit"
onPress={handleSubmit} />
    </View>
  );
};

const styles = StyleSheet.create({
  container: {
    flex: 1,
    justifyContent: 'center',
    alignItems: 'center',
  },
  input: {
    height: 40,
    borderColor: 'gray',
    borderWidth: 1,
    marginBottom: 20,
    width: '80%',
    paddingHorizontal: 10,
  },
});

export default App;
```

In this example, we have two `TextInput` components—one for the user's name and one for the email. The state for each input is managed separately, and the `handleSubmit` function logs the values when the form is submitted.

Handling Form Submissions

Handling form submissions typically involves taking the values entered by the user, validating them, and then performing an action, such as sending the data to a server or navigating to another screen.

1. **Handling Submit Button Press**: When the user presses a submit button, you can trigger a function to handle the submission of the form data. This function might involve validating the inputs and performing actions like sending data to an API.

   Example:

   javascript

```
const handleSubmit = () => {
  if (name === '' || email === '') {
    alert('Please fill in all fields');
  } else {
    console.log('Name:', name);
```

```
console.log('Email:', email);
// Send data to an API or navigate to
another screen
  }
};
```

2. **Clearing the Form After Submission**: After the form is submitted, you may want to clear the input fields. You can do this by resetting the state of each input field.

   Example:

   javascript

```
const handleSubmit = () => {
  if (name === '' || email === '') {
    alert('Please fill in all fields');
  } else {
    console.log('Form Submitted');
    setName('');  // Clear the name field
    setEmail('');  // Clear the email field
  }
};
```

Validating User Input

Validating user input is an important step in ensuring that the data entered into your form is correct and secure. React Native provides simple ways to handle validation, either by checking values directly in your code or using third-party libraries.

1. **Basic Validation**: You can perform basic validation directly within the `handleSubmit` function by checking that the fields are not empty, ensuring proper formats, or checking for specific constraints.

   Example (Basic validation for email format):

   javascript

   ```javascript
   const handleSubmit = () => {
     if (name === '' || email === '') {
       alert('Please fill in all fields');
     } else if (!/\S+@\S+\.\S+/.test(email))
   {   // Email regex check
       alert('Please enter a valid email');
     } else {
       console.log('Form Submitted');
       setName('');
       setEmail('');
     }
   };
   ```

2. **Using a Validation Library**: For more advanced validation, you can use libraries like **Formik** and **Yup**, which offer powerful form-handling and validation mechanisms for React Native.

   o **Formik** simplifies form handling by abstracting form logic, and **Yup** is commonly used with Formik for schema-based validation.

o Example with Formik and Yup:

```bash
npm install formik yup
```

3. Example (Form validation with Formik and Yup):
4. javascript
5.
6. import React from 'react';
7. import { View, TextInput, Button, Text } from 'react-native';
8. import { Formik } from 'formik';
9. import * as Yup from 'yup';
10.
11. const validationSchema = Yup.object().shape({
12.   name: Yup.string().required('Name is required'),
13.   email: Yup.string().email('Invalid email address').required('Email is required'),
14. });
15.
16. const App = () => {
17.   return (
18.   <Formik
19.   initialValues={{ name: '', email: '' }}
```
```

```
20.
   validationSchema={validationSchema}
21.       onSubmit={(values) => {
22.         console.log('Form     Submitted',
   values);
23.         }}
24.     >
25.        {({   handleChange,   handleSubmit,
   values, errors }) => (
26.          <View>
27.            <TextInput
28.              style={{     height:     40,
   borderColor:   'gray',   borderWidth:   1,
   marginBottom: 20 }}
29.              placeholder="Enter     your
   name"
30.              value={values.name}
31.
   onChangeText={handleChange('name')}
32.            />
33.            {errors.name && <Text style={{
   color: 'red' }}>{errors.name}</Text>}
34.
35.            <TextInput
36.              style={{     height:     40,
   borderColor:   'gray',   borderWidth:   1,
   marginBottom: 20 }}
37.              placeholder="Enter     your
   email"
```

```
38.                value={values.email}
39.
    onChangeText={handleChange('email')}
40.              />
41.              {errors.email && <Text style={{
    color: 'red' }}>{errors.email}</Text>}
42.
43.              <Button        title="Submit"
    onPress={handleSubmit} />
44.          </View>
45.        )}
46.      </Formik>
47.    );
48.  };
49.
50. export default App;
```

51. In this example, Formik handles the form state and submission, while Yup validates the fields based on the specified rules. Error messages are displayed if the input does not meet the validation criteria.

Conclusion

In this chapter, we covered the essential techniques for working with forms and user input in React Native. We explored how to create **TextInput** components and combine them into forms. We also discussed how to handle form submissions and validate user input. By mastering these techniques, you'll be able to build user-friendly forms and ensure that the data collected from users is accurate and reliable.

CHAPTER 9

HANDLING ASYNCHRONOUS DATA WITH FETCH AND AXIOS

In modern mobile applications, fetching data from remote servers is a common task. React Native provides simple and powerful ways to handle asynchronous operations, particularly for network requests. In this chapter, we'll cover the basics of asynchronous programming in React Native, how to make network requests using the built-in **fetch API**, and how **Axios**, a popular third-party library, can be used for more complex scenarios. We'll also discuss how to handle loading states and errors during data fetching.

Introduction to Asynchronous Programming in React Native

Asynchronous programming is crucial when working with operations like network requests, where responses are not immediately available. In React Native (and JavaScript in general), asynchronous operations are handled using **Promises** or **async/await** syntax.

- **Promises** represent a value that may be available now or in the future.

- **async/await** provides a more readable and convenient way to work with Promises.

React Native's network requests (using **fetch** or **Axios**) are asynchronous, meaning the app will not block the UI while waiting for the response from the server. Instead, React Native uses Promises to handle the data asynchronously.

Here's a simple example using `async/await`:

```javascript
const fetchData = async () => {
  try {
    const response = await fetch('https://jsonplaceholder.typicode.com/posts');
    const data = await response.json();
    console.log(data);
  } catch (error) {
    console.error('Error fetching data: ', error);
  }
};
```

In the example above, `fetchData` is an asynchronous function that waits for the server response, then parses it into JSON format, and finally logs the data to the console.

Using Fetch API to Make Network Requests

The **fetch API** is the built-in JavaScript method for making HTTP requests. It supports **GET**, **POST**, **PUT**, **DELETE**, and other HTTP methods.

1. **Making a GET Request with Fetch**: The most common operation is a **GET** request, which retrieves data from a remote server. Below is an example of how to use the `fetch` method to make a GET request in React Native:

   Example (Fetching Data with `fetch`):

   ```javascript
   import React, { useState, useEffect } from
   'react';
   import { View, Text, ActivityIndicator }
   from 'react-native';

   const App = () => {
     const [data, setData] = useState(null);
     const [loading, setLoading] =
   useState(true);
     const [error, setError] =
   useState(null);

     useEffect(() => {
       // Fetch data from API
   ```

```
const fetchData = async () => {
  try {
    const response = await
fetch('https://jsonplaceholder.typicode.c
om/posts');
    if (!response.ok) {
      throw new Error('Network
response was not ok');
    }
    const result = await
response.json();
    setData(result);
  } catch (error) {
    setError(error.message);
  } finally {
    setLoading(false);
  }
};

fetchData();
}, []);


if (loading) return <ActivityIndicator
size="large" color="#0000ff" />;
if (error) return <Text>Error:
{error}</Text>;


return (
  <View>
```

```
{data && data.map((item) => (
  <Text
key={item.id}>{item.title}</Text>
  )))}
 </View>
 );
};


export default App;
```

- o In this example:
  - The `useEffect` hook is used to fetch data when the component mounts.
  - The `ActivityIndicator` component is displayed while the data is being loaded.
  - Once the data is fetched, it's stored in the `data` state, and each post's title is displayed in the app.
  - If an error occurs, it's displayed on the screen.

2. **Making a POST Request with Fetch**: If you need to send data to a server, you can use the **POST** method. Here's how to send a POST request with `fetch`:

Example (Sending Data with `fetch`):

```
javascript
```

96

```
const postData = async () => {
  const        response        =        await
fetch('https://jsonplaceholder.typicode.c
om/posts', {
    method: 'POST',
    headers: {
      'Content-Type': 'application/json',
    },
    body: JSON.stringify({
      title: 'foo',
      body: 'bar',
      userId: 1,
    }),
  });
  const data = await response.json();
  console.log(data);
};
```

In this example, postData sends JSON data to the server
and logs the response. It uses the POST method and
includes the necessary headers for sending JSON data.

Introduction to Axios for More Advanced Requests

While fetch is a great tool, **Axios** is a more powerful and feature-
rich alternative for making HTTP requests in React Native. Axios
is a promise-based library that simplifies HTTP requests and
comes with several built-in features, such as handling request and

response transformations, intercepting requests, and automatic handling of JSON data.

1. **Installing Axios**: To use Axios in your project, you need to install it first:

```bash
bash

npm install axios
```

2. **Making a GET Request with Axios**: Axios simplifies the process of handling requests by automatically parsing JSON responses and handling errors in a more consistent manner. Here's an example of using Axios to fetch data:

Example (GET Request with Axios):

```javascript
javascript

import axios from 'axios';
import React, { useState, useEffect } from
'react';
import { View, Text, ActivityIndicator }
from 'react-native';

const App = () => {
  const [data, setData] = useState(null);
  const   [loading,    setLoading]    =
useState(true);
```

```
const      [error,      setError]      =
useState(null);

  useEffect(() => {
    axios

.get('https://jsonplaceholder.typicode.co
m/posts')
      .then((response) => {
        setData(response.data);
      })
      .catch((error) => {
        setError(error.message);
      })
      .finally(() => {
        setLoading(false);
      });
  }, []);


  if (loading) return <ActivityIndicator
size="large" color="#0000ff" />;
  if   (error)   return   <Text>Error:
{error}</Text>;

  return (
    <View>
      {data && data.map((item) => (
        <Text
key={item.id}>{item.title}</Text>
```

```
      ) ) }
    </View>
  );
};


export default App;
```

- o Axios's API is similar to `fetch` but simplifies error handling and automatic parsing of JSON data. It also supports additional features like request cancellation, custom headers, and interceptors for more advanced use cases.

3. **Making a POST Request with Axios**: Sending data via POST with Axios is very simple and requires only minor changes compared to `fetch`:

Example (POST Request with Axios):

javascript

```
const postData = () => {
  axios

.post('https://jsonplaceholder.typicode.c
om/posts', {
      title: 'foo',
      body: 'bar',
      userId: 1,
    })
```

```
    .then((response) => {
      console.log(response.data);
    })
    .catch((error) => {
      console.error(error);
    });
  };
```

Handling Loading States and Errors

When dealing with asynchronous requests, you need to properly manage loading states and errors to provide a good user experience.

1. **Loading State**:
   - Display a loading spinner or message while the data is being fetched. This lets the user know that something is happening in the background.
   - Use `ActivityIndicator` in React Native to show a loading spinner.

Example:

```javascript

if (loading) return <ActivityIndicator
size="large" color="#0000ff" />;
```

2. **Error Handling**:

101

- o Always handle errors gracefully. Use a `try/catch` block with `async/await` or `.catch()` with Promises to handle any issues that arise during the data-fetching process.
- o Display user-friendly error messages to the user, so they know if something went wrong.

Example:

```javascript

if (error) return <Text>Error: {error}</Text>;
```

Conclusion

In this chapter, we've explored how to handle asynchronous data fetching in React Native using the **fetch API** and **Axios**. You've learned how to make both **GET** and **POST** requests, handle loading states with `ActivityIndicator`, and manage errors effectively. By using these tools, you can interact with remote APIs, gather and display data, and provide users with a smooth, responsive experience. Whether you use `fetch` for simple tasks or Axios for more advanced scenarios, these techniques are essential for building modern, data-driven mobile apps.

CHAPTER 10

STYLING IN REACT NATIVE

Styling is a crucial part of building any mobile application, and React Native provides a variety of tools to help developers create beautiful and responsive user interfaces. In this chapter, we'll explore how to apply styles using **StyleSheet**, understand how the **Flexbox** layout system works, use third-party libraries like **Styled Components** for styling, and dive into techniques for making your app responsive across different device sizes.

Applying Styles Using StyleSheet

In React Native, the primary way to apply styles is through the **StyleSheet** API. The StyleSheet object is a performance-optimized way of creating styles in React Native. It works similarly to CSS in web development but with a few differences suited to mobile development.

1. **Basic Usage of StyleSheet**: React Native's StyleSheet.create() method is used to define a collection of styles that can be applied to various components. It offers a performance advantage by creating a single reference to the styles, which React Native can optimize when rendering.

Example:

```javascript

import React from 'react';
import { View, Text, StyleSheet } from
'react-native';

const App = () => {
  return (
    <View style={styles.container}>
      <Text style={styles.text}>Hello,
React Native!</Text>
    </View>
  );
};

const styles = StyleSheet.create({
  container: {
    flex: 1,
    justifyContent: 'center',
    alignItems: 'center',
    backgroundColor: '#f0f0f0',
  },
  text: {
    fontSize: 20,
    fontWeight: 'bold',
    color: 'blue',
  },
});
```

```
export default App;
```

- o In this example, the `container` style centers the `Text` element both horizontally and vertically using **Flexbox**. The `text` style changes the font size, weight, and color of the text.

2. **Dynamic Styling**: Sometimes you may need to apply styles dynamically, depending on component state or props. This can be done by conditionally assigning style objects.

Example (Dynamic Styling):

```
javascript
```

```
import React, { useState } from 'react';
import { View, Text, Button, StyleSheet }
from 'react-native';

const App = () => {
  const        [isRed,        setIsRed]        =
useState(false);

  return (
    <View style={styles.container}>
      <Text style={[styles.text, isRed &&
styles.redText]}>
        Hello, React Native!
```

```
    </Text>
    <Button       title="Toggle       Red"
onPress={() => setIsRed(!isRed)} />
  </View>
  );
};


const styles = StyleSheet.create({
  container: {
    flex: 1,
    justifyContent: 'center',
    alignItems: 'center',
    backgroundColor: '#f0f0f0',
  },
  text: {
    fontSize: 20,
    fontWeight: 'bold',
  },
  redText: {
    color: 'red',
  },
});


export default App;
```

- o In this example, the redText style is
  conditionally applied to the text when the isRed
  state is true.

Understanding Flexbox Layout System

Flexbox is a powerful layout system in React Native that helps you arrange UI elements on the screen. Flexbox is particularly useful when building mobile interfaces because it adapts well to different screen sizes and orientations.

1. **Flexbox Concepts**:
    o   **Main Axis**: The direction in which the flex items are laid out (either horizontally or vertically). You control the direction with the `flexDirection` property.
    o   **Cross Axis**: The perpendicular direction to the main axis. For example, if the main axis is horizontal, the cross axis is vertical.
    o   **Justify Content**: Aligns the children along the main axis (horizontal or vertical).
    o   **Align Items**: Aligns the children along the cross axis.

2. **Flexbox Properties**:
    o   `flexDirection`: Controls the main axis direction. Can be `row` (horizontal) or `column` (vertical).
    o   `justifyContent`: Aligns children along the main axis. Options include `flex-start`, `center`, `flex-end`, `space-between`, and `space-around`.

- o alignItems: **Aligns children along the cross axis. Options** include flex-start, center, flex-end, **and** stretch.
- o flex: **Defines how a component should grow or shrink relative to its siblings.**

Example:

```javascript

import React from 'react';
import { View, Text, StyleSheet } from 'react-native';

const App = () => {
  return (
    <View style={styles.container}>
      <Text       style={styles.text}>Item 1</Text>
      <Text       style={styles.text}>Item 2</Text>
      <Text       style={styles.text}>Item 3</Text>
    </View>
  );
};

const styles = StyleSheet.create({
  container: {
```

```
    flex: 1,
    flexDirection: 'row',  // Items will be
arranged horizontally
    justifyContent: 'space-around',    //
Items will be spaced evenly
    alignItems: 'center',  // Items will be
aligned vertically in the center
  },
  text: {
    fontSize: 20,
    fontWeight: 'bold',
  },
});

export default App;
```

o In this example, the `container` style arranges the `Text` elements horizontally (`flexDirection: 'row'`), centers them vertically (`alignItems: 'center'`), and spaces them evenly along the main axis (`justifyContent: 'space-around'`).

Using Third-Party Libraries for Styling (e.g., Styled Components)

While React Native provides built-in styling with **StyleSheet**, third-party libraries can offer more advanced and dynamic styling features. **Styled Components** is one such library that brings CSS-like styling to React Native.

1. **Installing Styled Components**: To use **Styled Components** in your React Native project, you first need to install it:

```bash
bash
```

```bash
npm install styled-components
```

2. **Using Styled Components**: **Styled Components** allows you to write component-level styles using tagged template literals, similar to how you would write CSS in a web app.

Example:

```javascript
javascript
```

```javascript
import React from 'react';
import styled from 'styled-components/native';
import { View, Text } from 'react-native';

const Container = styled.View`
  flex: 1;
  justify-content: center;
  align-items: center;
  background-color: #f0f0f0;
`;
```

110

```
const StyledText = styled.Text`
  font-size: 20px;
  font-weight: bold;
  color: blue;
`;

const App = () => {
  return (
    <Container>
      <StyledText>Hello    from    Styled
Components!</StyledText>
    </Container>
  );
};

export default App;
```

- o In this example, the `Container` and `StyledText` components are styled using **styled-components**. This approach is highly readable and keeps your styles organized directly with your components.

Responsive Design Techniques

Building responsive apps in React Native ensures that your app looks great on devices with different screen sizes and orientations. Here are some common techniques:

111

1. **Using `Dimensions` API**: The `Dimensions` API in React Native allows you to get the screen width and height, which you can use to adjust the layout of your app for different screen sizes.

Example:

```javascript
import React from 'react';
import { View, Text, StyleSheet, Dimensions } from 'react-native';

const { width, height } = Dimensions.get('window');

const App = () => {
  return (
    <View style={[styles.container, { width: width * 0.8 }]}>
      <Text style={styles.text}>Screen width: {width}</Text>
      <Text style={styles.text}>Screen height: {height}</Text>
    </View>
  );
};

const styles = StyleSheet.create({
```

```
container: {
    flex: 1,
    justifyContent: 'center',
    alignItems: 'center',
},
text: {
    fontSize: 20,
},
});
```

```
export default App;
```

o   In this example, the width of the container is set to 80% of the screen width, allowing it to adapt to different screen sizes.

2. **Using `flex` for Responsive Layouts**: Using `flex` in your layouts is a great way to ensure that components scale based on the screen size. Flexbox automatically adjusts items within a container based on the available space.

3. **Using Media Queries with `react-native-media-query`**: For more advanced responsiveness, you can use the `react-native-media-query` library to apply media queries, similar to CSS on the web.

Example:

```bash
```

```
npm install react-native-media-query
javascript

import { useMediaQuery } from 'react-
native-media-query';

const App = () => {
  const { isSmallDevice } = useMediaQuery({
    query: '(max-width: 400px)',
  });

  return (
    <View style={{ flex: 1 }}>
      <Text          style={{          fontSize:
isSmallDevice ? 14 : 20 }}>
        {isSmallDevice ? 'Small Device' :
'Large Device'}
      </Text>
    </View>
  );
};
```

o   This example applies different font sizes based on
    the device's width, providing a responsive design.

Conclusion

In this chapter, we've explored how to apply styles in React Native using the **StyleSheet** API, the power of **Flexbox** for layout management, and how third-party libraries like **Styled Components** can help streamline styling with a CSS-like syntax. Additionally, we learned key techniques for creating responsive designs that adapt to different screen sizes and orientations using the **Dimensions** API, **flexbox**, and media queries.

Mastering these styling techniques will help you build visually appealing, responsive, and user-friendly mobile apps in React Native.

CHAPTER 11

WORKING WITH IMAGES AND MEDIA

In React Native, handling images and media files is essential for building rich and interactive mobile applications. This chapter covers how to display images using the **Image** component, how to work with images from both the web and local assets, and how to handle media files such as videos and audio.

Displaying Images with the Image Component

The **Image** component in React Native is used to display both local and remote images. It's highly customizable and provides various properties to control how images are rendered.

1. **Basic Usage of the Image Component**: The `Image` component requires the `source` prop, which specifies the image's location. This can either be a URI (for remote images) or a local file path (for assets stored in the project).

   Example (Displaying a Local Image):

   ```
   javascript
   ```

116

```
import React from 'react';
import { View, Image, StyleSheet } from
'react-native';

const App = () => {
  return (
    <View style={styles.container}>
      <Image

source={require('./assets/myImage.png')}
// Local image
        style={styles.image}
      />
    </View>
  );
};

const styles = StyleSheet.create({
  container: {
    flex: 1,
    justifyContent: 'center',
    alignItems: 'center',
  },
  image: {
    width: 200,
    height: 200,
  },
});
```

117

```
export default App;
```

- o In this example, the `Image` component is used to render a local image located in the `assets` folder. The `style` prop is used to define the size of the image.

2. **Handling Remote Images**: You can display images that are hosted on remote servers by providing a URL to the `source` prop.

Example (Displaying a Remote Image):

```javascript
import React from 'react';
import { View, Image, StyleSheet } from
'react-native';

const App = () => {
  return (
    <View style={styles.container}>
      <Image
        source={{                          uri:
'https://example.com/image.jpg'  }}      //
Remote image
        style={styles.image}
      />
    </View>
```

```
  );
};


const styles = StyleSheet.create({
  container: {
    flex: 1,
    justifyContent: 'center',
    alignItems: 'center',
  },
  image: {
    width: 200,
    height: 200,
  },
});


export default App;
```

- o Here, we are displaying a remote image by passing a URL as the `uri` inside the `source` object.

3. **Advanced Image Properties**: The **Image** component offers several other properties for handling images:
   - o `resizeMode`: Controls how the image should be resized to fit the container. It can be one of the following values: `cover`, `contain`, or `stretch`.
   - o `onLoad`: A function called when the image finishes loading.

     o   `onError`: A function called when the image fails to load.

Example (Image with Resize Mode):

```javascript
```

```
<Image
  source={{                              uri:
'https://example.com/image.jpg' }}
  style={styles.image}
  resizeMode="contain"
/>
```

Handling Images from the Web and Local Assets

1. **Handling Local Assets**:

     o   For local images (images that are part of your app's assets), use the `require()` method to reference the image. React Native bundles the image with your app's assets when the app is built.

     o   Place your images in the `assets` folder (or any other directory within the project) and use `require()` to include them in the app.

Example:

```javascript
```

```
<Image
source={require('./assets/localImage.png'
)} style={styles.image} />
```

2. **Handling Remote Images**:

   o   Remote images are accessed using a URL. React
       Native automatically fetches the image from the
       server and displays it when the app is loaded.

   o   You can pass a URL to the `uri` field in the
       `source` prop, as shown earlier.

Example:

```javascript
```

```
<Image            source={{         uri:
'https://example.com/image.jpg'           }}
style={styles.image} />
```

3. **Image Caching**: React Native doesn't cache remote
   images by default, which could lead to performance
   issues if an image is fetched repeatedly. To manage image
   caching, you can use third-party libraries like **react-
   native-fast-image** for efficient caching and faster
   loading.

Working with Videos and Audio Files

Working with videos and audio files is common in many apps, such as those that display tutorials, allow media playback, or include sound effects. React Native provides components and libraries to handle media playback.

1. **Displaying and Playing Videos**: React Native has a built-in component called **Video**, but you can also use third-party libraries such as **react-native-video** for more advanced features.

   o **Install react-native-video**:

   ```bash
   npm install react-native-video
   ```

   o Example (Playing a Video):

   ```javascript
   import React from 'react';
   import { View, StyleSheet } from 'react-native';
   import Video from 'react-native-video';

   const App = () => {
     return (
   ```

122

```jsx
    <View style={styles.container}>
      <Video
        source={{              uri:
'https://www.w3schools.com/html/mov
ie.mp4' }}

style={styles.backgroundVideo}
        controls={true}
        resizeMode="contain"
      />
    </View>
  );
};

const styles = StyleSheet.create({
  container: {
    flex: 1,
    justifyContent: 'center',
    alignItems: 'center',
  },
  backgroundVideo: {
    width: '100%',
    height: 300,
  },
});

export default App;
```

o In this example, **react-native-video** is used to display and control video playback. The `controls={true}` prop adds default video controls (play, pause, etc.).

2. **Playing Audio**: React Native doesn't have a built-in component for audio, but you can use the **react-native-sound** library or other third-party libraries to play audio files.

   o **Install react-native-sound**:

   bash

   ```
   npm install react-native-sound
   ```

   o Example (Playing Audio):

   javascript

   ```
   import React, { useState } from
   'react';
   import { Button, View } from 'react-
   native';
   import Sound from 'react-native-
   sound';

   const App = () => {
     const [sound, setSound] =
   useState(null);
   ```

124

```
const playSound = () => {
    const       s       =       new
Sound('https://www.soundhelix.com/e
xamples/mp3/SoundHelix-Song-1.mp3',
null, (error) => {
        if (error) {
            console.log('Error    loading
sound:', error);
            return;
        }
        s.play();
    });
    setSound(s);
};


return (
    <View>
        <Button    title="Play    Sound"
onPress={playSound} />
    </View>
    );
};


export default App;
```

o   In this example, the react-native-sound
    library is used to play an audio file from a remote
    URL when the button is pressed.

3. **Handling Audio Playback Controls**: You can control audio playback (e.g., play, pause, stop) and handle events (such as when the sound finishes playing) using the available methods and events provided by **react-native-sound** or other audio libraries.

Conclusion

In this chapter, we covered how to handle **images** and **media files** in React Native. You learned how to display images using the **Image** component, handle both local and remote images, and manage advanced image features like resizing. We also explored how to work with **videos** using **react-native-video** and play **audio** files using libraries like **react-native-sound**.

By mastering image and media handling, you'll be able to add rich media content to your React Native apps, providing a more engaging and interactive user experience. Whether you're displaying photos, playing videos, or streaming audio, these tools will allow you to integrate media into your mobile applications seamlessly.

CHAPTER 12

HANDLING DEVICE FEATURES (CAMERA, LOCATION, ETC.)

In this chapter, we'll explore how to access device features like the **camera** and **location** in React Native. These features allow your app to interact with the device hardware, creating more dynamic and engaging user experiences. We will also cover how to handle permissions, which is an essential part of accessing sensitive device features. Finally, we'll look at a real-world example: building a simple photo app that uses the camera to capture photos.

Accessing Device Features Like Camera and Location

1. **Accessing the Camera**: React Native doesn't provide a built-in camera component, but you can use third-party libraries to access the camera. One of the most popular libraries is **react-native-camera** or **expo-camera** if you are using Expo. These libraries provide easy-to-use APIs for capturing photos and videos.

   o **Using react-native-camera**: First, install the necessary library:

   bash

```
npm install react-native-camera
```

After installation, link the library (for non-Expo users):

```
bash
```

```
react-native    link    react-native-camera
```

Here's an example of how to use **react-native-camera** to take a photo:

Example (Camera Access with react-native-camera):

```
javascript
```

```javascript
import React, { useState } from 'react';
import { View, Button, Image, StyleSheet } from 'react-native';
import { RNCamera } from 'react-native-camera';

const CameraApp = () => {
  const [photoUri, setPhotoUri] = useState(null);
```

```
const takePicture = async (camera)
=> {
  const    data    =    await
camera.takePictureAsync();
  setPhotoUri(data.uri);
};


return (
  <View style={styles.container}>
    <RNCamera
      style={styles.camera}

type={RNCamera.Constants.Type.back}

flashMode={RNCamera.Constants.Flash
Mode.on}
      >
      {(( camera, status,
recordAudioPermissionStatus }) => (
        <>
          <Button title="Take
Photo"    onPress={()    =>
takePicture(camera)} />
          {photoUri && <Image
source={{ uri: photoUri }}
style={styles.photo} />}
        </>
      )}
    </RNCamera>
```

```
    </View>
  );
};


const styles = StyleSheet.create({
  container: {
    flex: 1,
    justifyContent: 'center',
    alignItems: 'center',
  },
  camera: {
    width: '100%',
    height: '100%',
  },
  photo: {
    width: 200,
    height: 200,
    marginTop: 20,
  },
});


export default CameraApp;
```

- In this example, the `RNCamera` component is used to display the camera view. The `takePicture` function captures a photo when the user presses the "Take Photo" button. The captured

130

photo's URI is then displayed on the screen.

o **Permissions for Camera Access**: To use the camera, you need to request the appropriate permissions from the user. React Native provides an API to request permissions, and you can also use libraries like **react-native-permissions** to handle permissions more efficiently.

2. **Accessing the Location**: React Native allows you to access the device's GPS to get the current location of the user using the **Geolocation API** or libraries like **react-native-geolocation-service**.

o **Using the Geolocation API**: React Native's built-in **Geolocation API** can be used to get the user's current position. Here's an example of how to retrieve the location:

Example (Getting the Location with Geolocation API):

```javascript
import React, { useState, useEffect
} from 'react';
import { View, Text, Button,
StyleSheet } from 'react-native';

const LocationApp = () => {
```

```
const [location, setLocation] =
useState(null);

const getLocation = () => {

navigator.geolocation.getCurrentPos
ition(
    (position) => {

setLocation(position.coords);
    },
    (error) => {
      console.log(error);
    },
    { enableHighAccuracy: true,
timeout: 20000, maximumAge: 1000 }
  );
};

return (
  <View style={styles.container}>
    <Button title="Get Location"
onPress={getLocation} />
    {location && (
      <Text>
        Latitude:
{location.latitude}, Longitude:
{location.longitude}
      </Text>
```

```
        ) }
      </View>
    );
};


const styles = StyleSheet.create({
  container: {
    flex: 1,
    justifyContent: 'center',
    alignItems: 'center',
  },
});


export default LocationApp;
```

- In this example, the `getLocation` function uses the **navigator.geolocation.getCurrentPosition** method to fetch the current geographic position of the device. The latitude and longitude are displayed on the screen after the button is pressed.

o **Permissions for Location Access**: Similar to camera access, you need to request permission to access the user's location. React Native provides a **PermissionsAndroid** API for Android and **requestLocationPermission** for iOS, or you can use third-party libraries to handle permissions.

Using Permissions in React Native

Handling permissions is crucial in React Native because accessing device features such as the camera and location requires explicit user consent. React Native provides a built-in **PermissionsAndroid** API for Android and **React Native Permissions** (via third-party libraries) for both Android and iOS.

1. **Requesting Camera and Location Permissions**:

   Example (Requesting Permissions using `react-native-permissions`):

   ```bash
   npm install react-native-permissions
   ```

   ```javascript
   import React, { useEffect, useState } from 'react';
   import { View, Text, Button, StyleSheet } from 'react-native';
   import { check, request, PERMISSIONS, RESULTS } from 'react-native-permissions';

   const PermissionApp = () => {
     const [cameraPermission, setCameraPermission] = useState(null);
   ```

```
useEffect(() => {
  requestCameraPermission();
}, []);

const requestCameraPermission = async ()
=> {
  const       result       =       await
request(PERMISSIONS.ANDROID.CAMERA);
  setCameraPermission(result);
};

return (
  <View style={styles.container}>
    <Text>Camera              Permission:
{cameraPermission}</Text>
    <Button     title="Request      Camera
Permission"
onPress={requestCameraPermission} />
  </View>
);
};

const styles = StyleSheet.create({
  container: {
    flex: 1,
    justifyContent: 'center',
    alignItems: 'center',
  },
});
```

```
export default PermissionApp;
```

- o In this example, the `request` method from the `react-native-permissions` library is used to request camera permissions. The result is displayed to the user, showing whether permission was granted or denied.

2. **Handling Permissions on iOS**: On iOS, you need to configure the **Info.plist** file with the appropriate keys to request permission for camera and location access. For example, add the following to the **Info.plist** for camera access:

xml

```
<key>NSCameraUsageDescription</key>
<string>We need access to your camera for taking photos</string>
```

Similarly, for location access, you need to add:

xml

```
<key>NSLocationWhenInUseUsageDescription<
/key>
<string>We need access to your location to show nearby places</string>
```

Real-World Example: Building a Photo App

Now that we've explored accessing the camera and location, let's combine these features into a real-world example: building a simple **photo app** that allows the user to capture a photo and save its location.

1. **App Overview**:
   - The app will use the camera to take a picture.
   - After capturing the photo, the app will display the photo along with the GPS coordinates (latitude and longitude) of where the photo was taken.

2. **Code Example**:

javascript

```javascript
import React, { useState } from 'react';
import { View, Text, Button, Image,
StyleSheet } from 'react-native';
import { RNCamera } from 'react-native-
camera';
import Geolocation from 'react-native-
geolocation-service';

const PhotoApp = () => {
    const [photoUri, setPhotoUri] =
useState(null);
    const [location, setLocation] =
useState(null);
```

137

```
const takePicture = async (camera) => {
  const      data      =      await
camera.takePictureAsync();
  setPhotoUri(data.uri);

  // Get the location after taking the
photo
  Geolocation.getCurrentPosition(
    (position) => {
      setLocation(position.coords);
    },
    (error) => {
      console.log(error);
    },
    { enableHighAccuracy: true, timeout:
20000, maximumAge: 1000 }
  );
};

return (
  <View style={styles.container}>
    <RNCamera
      style={styles.camera}

type={RNCamera.Constants.Type.back}

flashMode={RNCamera.Constants.FlashMode.o
n}
```

```
        >
        {({ camera }) => (
          <>
            <Button    title="Take    Photo"
onPress={() => takePicture(camera)} />
            {photoUri && <Image source={{
uri: photoUri }} style={styles.photo} />}
            {location && (
              <Text>
                Location:
{location.latitude}, {location.longitude}
              </Text>
            )}
          </>
        )}
      </RNCamera>
    </View>
  );
};

const styles = StyleSheet.create({
  container: {
    flex: 1,
    justifyContent: 'center',
    alignItems: 'center',
  },
  camera: {
    width: '100%',
    height: '100%',
```

```
    },
    photo: {
      width: 200,
      height: 200,
      marginTop: 20,
    },
});


export default PhotoApp;
```

  o In this example, we combine the **RNCamera** to
     capture photos and **Geolocation** to fetch the
     location coordinates. After the photo is taken, the
     location is displayed along with the photo.

Conclusion

In this chapter, we explored how to access device features like the
camera and **location** in React Native. We learned how to use
react-native-camera for capturing photos, how to access the
device's location using **Geolocation**, and how to handle
permissions for these device features. Finally, we built a simple
photo app that captures a photo and displays the location where it
was taken.

By mastering these device features, you can create more
interactive and personalized mobile applications that leverage the
full capabilities of the user's device.

CHAPTER 13

ADVANCED NAVIGATION PATTERNS

In this chapter, we will explore some advanced navigation patterns in React Native, specifically **deep linking**, **nested navigation**, and **dynamic routing**. We'll also cover how to manage navigation state effectively to handle complex navigation scenarios in your app. These advanced techniques will allow you to create a more flexible and intuitive navigation experience for your users.

Deep Linking and Navigation with URL Schemes

Deep linking allows you to open a specific screen or part of your app via a URL, either from an external app, a browser, or a notification. It's useful for cases like handling links in emails, SMS, or push notifications, as well as integrating with web-based applications.

1. **Setting Up Deep Linking in React Navigation**: React Navigation supports deep linking out of the box. Deep linking works by mapping the URL path to the screen in your app. You can define how different URL paths should be handled by React Navigation using a linking configuration.

141

Example:

```javascript

import * as React from 'react';
import { NavigationContainer } from
'@react-navigation/native';
import { createStackNavigator } from
'@react-navigation/stack';
import HomeScreen from
'./screens/HomeScreen';
import ProfileScreen from
'./screens/ProfileScreen';

const Stack = createStackNavigator();

const App = () => {
  const linking = {
    prefixes: ['myapp://'],
    config: {
      screens: {
        Home: '',
        Profile: 'profile/:id',      //
Dynamic route parameter
      },
    },
  };

  return (
```

```
<NavigationContainer
linking={linking}>
    <Stack.Navigator>
        <Stack.Screen          name="Home"
component={HomeScreen} />
        <Stack.Screen          name="Profile"
component={ProfileScreen} />
    </Stack.Navigator>
  </NavigationContainer>
  );
};

export default App;
```

o **Explanation**:

- The linking configuration defines the URL schemes that the app will handle (myapp:// in this case).

- The Profile screen is defined to handle a dynamic URL like myapp://profile/123, where 123 is the user ID passed in the URL.

- When a user navigates to myapp://profile/123, React Navigation will open the Profile screen and pass 123 as a parameter.

2. **Opening App with a Deep Link**: To test deep linking, you can open the app with a URL directly from the device or simulator. On Android, use the `adb` command:

```bash
adb    shell    am    start    -W    -a
android.intent.action.VIEW            -d
"myapp://profile/123" com.myapp
```

On iOS, you can use the following:

```bash
xcrun    simctl    openurl    booted
myapp://profile/123
```

3. **Handling External Deep Links**: If you want your app to handle incoming links from external sources, you can configure the app to listen for deep links. React Native provides **Linking** API for this:

Example:

```javascript
import { Linking } from 'react-native';
```

```javascript
Linking.addEventListener('url', (event) =>
{
  console.log('Deep      link      received:',
event.url);
});

// In your app's componentDidMount
Linking.getInitialURL().then((url) => {
  if (url) {
    console.log('App      opened      from      deep
link:', url);
  }
});
```

Nested Navigation and Dynamic Routing

As apps grow in complexity, you may need to handle more sophisticated navigation patterns, such as **nested navigation** or **dynamic routing**. Nested navigation refers to having navigation stacks inside other navigation stacks, which allows for more granular control over the app's navigation structure.

1. **Nested Navigation**: You can nest navigation stacks, tabs, or drawers inside each other. React Navigation makes it easy to organize your app with multiple levels of navigation.

   Example (Nested Stack and Tab Navigation):

   ```
   javascript
   ```

```
import * as React from 'react';
import { NavigationContainer } from
'@react-navigation/native';
import { createStackNavigator } from
'@react-navigation/stack';
import { createBottomTabNavigator } from
'@react-navigation/bottom-tabs';
import HomeScreen from
'./screens/HomeScreen';
import ProfileScreen from
'./screens/ProfileScreen';
import SettingsScreen from
'./screens/SettingsScreen';

const Stack = createStackNavigator();
const Tab = createBottomTabNavigator();

const TabNavigator = () => (
  <Tab.Navigator>
    <Tab.Screen                name="Home"
component={HomeScreen} />
    <Tab.Screen               name="Profile"
component={ProfileScreen} />
  </Tab.Navigator>
);

const App = () => {
  return (
```

```
<NavigationContainer>
  <Stack.Navigator>
    <Stack.Screen          name="Tabs"
component={TabNavigator} />
    <Stack.Screen         name="Settings"
component={SettingsScreen} />
  </Stack.Navigator>
</NavigationContainer>
);
};

export default App;
```

- o **Explanation**:
  - The TabNavigator is nested within the StackNavigator. This allows you to create an app where the Home and Profile screens are accessible via tab navigation, and the Settings screen is accessible via stack navigation.
  - Nested navigation allows you to combine multiple types of navigation in one app.

2. **Dynamic Routing**: Dynamic routing allows you to create routes based on parameters or conditions. This is useful for apps where navigation depends on user input or specific conditions.

Example (Dynamic Screen Routing):

```javascript
const App = () => {
  return (
    <NavigationContainer>
      <Stack.Navigator>
        <Stack.Screen              name="Home"
component={HomeScreen} />
        <Stack.Screen            name="Details"
component={DetailsScreen} />
        <Stack.Screen
          name="UserProfile"
          component={UserProfileScreen}
          initialParams={{ userId: 123 }}
// Dynamically pass parameters
        />
      </Stack.Navigator>
    </NavigationContainer>
  );
};
```

o   In this example, the UserProfileScreen can
dynamically accept parameters like userId and
render content based on that value. You can also
use navigation parameters to conditionally
navigate between screens.

Managing Navigation State

In complex apps, managing navigation state is critical, especially when dealing with deep links, nested navigation, and dynamic routing. React Navigation provides a robust mechanism for managing navigation state, enabling you to maintain a consistent flow and restore navigation history if needed.

1. **Navigating with State**: You can pass and manage state across screens using **navigation parameters**. React Navigation provides the `route` prop to access these parameters in the screen component.

   Example (Passing and Accessing Parameters):

   ```javascript
   const HomeScreen = ({ navigation }) => {
     const navigateToDetails = () => {
       navigation.navigate('Details',         {
   itemId: 86 });
     };

     return (
       <Button    title="Go    to    Details"
   onPress={navigateToDetails} />
     );
   };
   ```

```
const DetailsScreen = ({ route }) => {
  const { itemId } = route.params;    //
Access passed parameter

  return <Text>Item ID: {itemId}</Text>;
};
```

2. **Persisting Navigation State**: React Navigation provides a way to persist navigation state, which is especially useful when users navigate away from the app and later return, or when the app is relaunched.

   To enable state persistence, you can use the **state persistence** feature:

```javascript
import { NavigationContainer } from
'@react-navigation/native';
import { createStackNavigator } from
'@react-navigation/stack';

const Stack = createStackNavigator();

const App = () => {
  return (
    <NavigationContainer>
      <Stack.Navigator>
```

```
        <Stack.Screen          name="Home"
component={HomeScreen} />
        <Stack.Screen          name="Details"
component={DetailsScreen} />
      </Stack.Navigator>
    </NavigationContainer>
  );
};
```

React Navigation will automatically persist the navigation state when the app is closed and reopened. If you need more control, you can implement custom state persistence mechanisms using libraries such as **redux-persist** or by saving navigation state in AsyncStorage.

3. **Resetting Navigation State**: In some cases, you may want to reset the navigation state completely, such as after a successful login or when the user logs out. React Navigation provides the `reset` method to achieve this.

Example (Resetting Navigation State):

```javascript
const resetToHome = () => {
  navigation.reset({
    index: 0,
    routes: [{ name: 'Home' }],
  });
```

```
};
```

    o This will reset the navigation stack and ensure that the `Home` screen becomes the first screen when the app is navigated back to.

Conclusion

In this chapter, we explored advanced navigation patterns in React Native, including **deep linking**, **nested navigation**, and **dynamic routing**. We also covered how to manage navigation state effectively, including passing parameters between screens, persisting state, and resetting navigation when necessary.

By mastering these advanced navigation techniques, you can create more sophisticated, user-friendly apps with complex navigation flows, ensuring that users can smoothly navigate between various screens, even with dynamic content or external links.

CHAPTER 14

USING REDUX FOR STATE MANAGEMENT

In complex applications, managing state across different components can become challenging. **Redux** is a state management library that helps you manage global state in a predictable and efficient way. In this chapter, we will introduce Redux and demonstrate how to integrate it into your React Native application for global state management. We will cover key concepts such as **actions, reducers, stores**, and how to connect Redux with React Native components.

Introduction to Redux for Global State Management

Redux is a popular JavaScript library that helps manage the state of an application. It follows a **predictable state container** pattern, which allows you to manage the application state centrally. Redux works by keeping the application state in a **store** and providing a set of **actions** and **reducers** to update that state.

The primary motivation for using Redux in React Native (or React) apps is to manage global state, making it easy to share data between components without passing props down the component tree.

1. **Core Concepts in Redux**:
   - **Store**: A store is a centralized place that holds the entire application state. The state is immutable, and the only way to change it is by dispatching actions.
   - **Actions**: Actions are plain JavaScript objects that describe what happened in the app. They must have a `type` property, which describes the type of action, and can optionally include a `payload` containing any data needed for the update.
   - **Reducers**: Reducers are pure functions that specify how the state should change in response to an action. A reducer takes the current state and the dispatched action as arguments and returns the new state.

Actions, Reducers, and Stores

1. **Actions**: Actions are the messages that tell the app what to do. They describe an event or a change in the app's state. Each action must have a `type` property, and it may also include additional data.

Example of an action:

```javascript

const incrementAction = {
```

154

```
type: 'INCREMENT', // Action type
payload: 1, // Data passed to the reducer
(optional)
};

const decrementAction = {
  type: 'DECREMENT',
  payload: 1,
};
```

2. **Reducers**: Reducers are responsible for handling actions and updating the state accordingly. They are pure functions that take the current state and action as arguments and return a new state.

Example of a simple reducer:

javascript

```
const initialState = {
  count: 0,
};

const   counterReducer   =   (state   =
initialState, action) => {
  switch (action.type) {
    case 'INCREMENT':
      return   {   ...state,   count:
state.count + action.payload };
```

```
case 'DECREMENT':
    return    {    ...state,    count:
state.count - action.payload };
    default:
      return state;
  }
};
```

- o In this example, `counterReducer` listens for INCREMENT and DECREMENT actions and updates the `count` in the state accordingly.

3. **Store**: The **store** holds the application's state and provides methods to dispatch actions and subscribe to changes in the state. The store is created using the `createStore` function from Redux.

Example of creating a store:

```javascript

import { createStore } from 'redux';

const store = createStore(counterReducer);
```

- o Here, `createStore(counterReducer)` creates a store with the `counterReducer` managing the state. The store holds the state and provides a method to dispatch actions to update it.

Connecting Redux to React Native Components

Once you have the store, actions, and reducers set up, you need to connect Redux with your React Native components to allow them to access and update the state.

1. **Installing Redux and React-Redux**: React-Redux is the official library that helps connect Redux to React Native (or React) components. To use Redux in your React Native app, you'll need to install both `redux` and `react-redux`.

   bash

   ```
   npm install redux react-redux
   ```

2. **Creating the Redux Store**: In a typical React Native application, you'll create the Redux store in a separate file and then provide it to the entire app using the **Provider** component from `react-redux`.

   Example (Setting Up Redux Store):

   javascript

   ```
   import React from 'react';
   import { createStore } from 'redux';
   import { Provider } from 'react-redux';
   ```

```
import counterReducer from './reducers';
// Import your reducers
import App from './App';

const store = createStore(counterReducer);

const Root = () => (
  <Provider store={store}>
    <App />
  </Provider>
);

export default Root;
```

      o   Here, the **Provider** component makes the Redux store available to all components in the app. The store is passed as a prop to the Provider, which ensures that the state is accessible to child components.

3. **Accessing State in Components (Using useSelector):** The **useSelector** hook is used to read the current state in your components. It allows you to select the specific piece of the state that you want to use.

Example (Reading the State):

```
javascript
```

```
import React from 'react';
```

```
import { useSelector } from 'react-redux';
import { View, Text } from 'react-native';

const CounterDisplay = () => {
  const count = useSelector((state) =>
state.count);

  return (
    <View>
      <Text>Current Count: {count}</Text>
    </View>
  );
};

export default CounterDisplay;
```

- o In this example, useSelector is used to access
  the count value from the Redux store and
  display it in the component.

4. **Dispatching Actions (Using useDispatch)**: The
   useDispatch hook is used to send actions to the Redux
   store. You call the dispatch function returned by
   useDispatch to send an action to the store and update
   the state.

Example (Dispatching Actions):

javascript

```
import React from 'react';
import { useDispatch } from 'react-redux';
import { View, Button } from 'react-
native';

const CounterControls = () => {
  const dispatch = useDispatch();

  const increment = () => {
    dispatch({ type: 'INCREMENT', payload:
1 });
  };

  const decrement = () => {
    dispatch({ type: 'DECREMENT', payload:
1 });
  };

  return (
    <View>
      <Button          title="Increment"
onPress={increment} />
      <Button          title="Decrement"
onPress={decrement} />
    </View>
  );
};

export default CounterControls;
```

o In this example, the `increment` and `decrement` functions dispatch the respective actions to update the state in the Redux store.

Putting It All Together: A Counter App Example

Let's combine everything into a simple **counter app** that uses Redux for state management.

1. **App Component**:

```javascript
import React from 'react';
import { View, Text, Button, StyleSheet } from 'react-native';
import { useSelector, useDispatch } from 'react-redux';

const App = () => {
  const count = useSelector((state) => state.count);
  const dispatch = useDispatch();

  const increment = () => {
    dispatch({ type: 'INCREMENT', payload: 1 });
  };
```

```
const decrement = () => {
  dispatch({ type: 'DECREMENT', payload:
1 });
  };


  return (
    <View style={styles.container}>
      <Text    style={styles.text}>Counter:
{count}</Text>
      <Button            title="Increment"
onPress={increment} />
      <Button            title="Decrement"
onPress={decrement} />
    </View>
  );
};


const styles = StyleSheet.create({
  container: {
    flex: 1,
    justifyContent: 'center',
    alignItems: 'center',
  },
  text: {
    fontSize: 30,
    fontWeight: 'bold',
  },
});
```

```
export default App;
```

2. **Reducer**:

```javascript

const initialState = {
  count: 0,
};

const counterReducer = (state = initialState, action) => {
  switch (action.type) {
    case 'INCREMENT':
      return { ...state, count: state.count + action.payload };
    case 'DECREMENT':
      return { ...state, count: state.count - action.payload };
    default:
      return state;
  }
};

export default counterReducer;
```

3. **Connecting Redux to the App**:
   o Wrap the app in a **Provider** and pass the store.

```javascript
```

```
import { createStore } from 'redux';
import { Provider } from 'react-redux';
import counterReducer from './reducers';
// Your reducer file
import App from './App';

const store = createStore(counterReducer);

const Root = () => (
  <Provider store={store}>
    <App />
  </Provider>
);

export default Root;
```

Conclusion

In this chapter, we covered the basics of **Redux** and how to use it for state management in a React Native app. We learned about **actions**, **reducers**, and **stores**, and how to connect Redux to React Native components using the **useSelector** and **useDispatch** hooks. By using Redux, we can manage global state in a predictable and scalable way, especially in larger applications where state needs to be shared between multiple components.

With Redux, you can build more complex and dynamic applications, ensuring that your app's state is predictable, centralized, and easily manageable.

CHAPTER 15

MANAGING DATA WITH ASYNCSTORAGE AND DATABASES

In mobile applications, it's essential to handle data persistence, so users can store and retrieve data even when they close or restart the app. React Native provides a variety of ways to store data locally, including **AsyncStorage**, **SQLite**, and **Realm**. In this chapter, we will explore how to use these tools for local data storage and databases. We'll also walk through a real-world example of saving user preferences.

Introduction to AsyncStorage for Local Data Storage

AsyncStorage is a simple, asynchronous, and persistent key-value storage system that allows you to save data on the device. It is ideal for storing lightweight data, such as user settings, app preferences, or small pieces of information. While **AsyncStorage** is suitable for small data storage, it's not recommended for storing large datasets.

1. **Installing AsyncStorage**: AsyncStorage was previously part of React Native, but it has since been moved to a

separate library. To use it, you need to install the @react-native-async-storage/async-storage package:

```bash

npm    install    @react-native-async-storage/async-storage
```

2. **Using AsyncStorage**: AsyncStorage is asynchronous, meaning that it works with Promises and can be used with async/await syntax for better readability.

   Example (Saving and Retrieving Data with AsyncStorage):

```javascript

import React, { useState, useEffect } from 'react';
import { View, Text, Button, AsyncStorage } from 'react-native';

const App = () => {
  const [userName, setUserName] = useState('');

  // Save data to AsyncStorage
  const saveData = async () => {
```

```
    try {
      await
AsyncStorage.setItem('@user_name',   'John
Doe');
    } catch (error) {
      console.log('Error  saving  data:  ',
error);
    }
  };


  // Retrieve data from AsyncStorage
  const getData = async () => {
    try {
      const      value      =      await
AsyncStorage.getItem('@user_name');
      if (value !== null) {
        setUserName(value);  //  Set  the
retrieved value to state
      }
    } catch (error) {
      console.log('Error  retrieving  data:
', error);
    }
  };


  useEffect(() => {
    getData(); // Retrieve data on initial
render
  }, []);
```

```
return (
  <View>
    <Text>User Name: {userName || 'No
name stored'}</Text>
    <Button    title="Save    Name"
onPress={saveData} />
  </View>
  );
};


export default App;
```

- o In this example:
  - ▪ We use `AsyncStorage.setItem()` to store the `userName`.
  - ▪ We retrieve the stored value using `AsyncStorage.getItem()` and display it in the app.
  - ▪ The data persists even after the app is closed and reopened.

3. **Common AsyncStorage Methods**:
   - o `setItem(key, value)`: Saves data with the given key.
   - o `getItem(key)`: Retrieves data stored under the specified key.
   - o `removeItem(key)`: Removes the stored value for the given key.

169

o   `clear()`: Clears all data stored in AsyncStorage.

4. **Limitations of AsyncStorage**:

    o   AsyncStorage is intended for lightweight data storage, not for storing large or complex datasets like images or files.

    o   For larger data, you might want to consider using local databases like **SQLite** or **Realm**.

Using SQLite and Realm for Local Databases

For more complex data storage needs, such as relational data or large datasets, **SQLite** and **Realm** are better choices. These databases offer more advanced features and allow you to manage data more efficiently.

1. **Using SQLite**: SQLite is a relational database that works well for apps that need to store structured data with relationships between entities (e.g., users, products, orders). React Native uses the **react-native-sqlite-storage** library to integrate SQLite.

    o   **Installing SQLite**:

    ```bash
    npm install react-native-sqlite-storage
    ```

    o   **Example (Using SQLite)**:

170

```javascript
javascript

import React, { useEffect } from 'react';
import { View, Text, Button } from 'react-native';
import SQLite from 'react-native-sqlite-storage';

const db = SQLite.openDatabase(
  { name: 'test.db', location: 'default' },
  () => console.log('Database opened'),
  (err) => console.log('Database error: ', err)
);

const App = () => {
  useEffect(() => {
    // Create a table
    db.transaction((tx) => {
      tx.executeSql(
        'CREATE TABLE IF NOT EXISTS users (id INTEGER PRIMARY KEY AUTOINCREMENT, name TEXT)',
        [],
        () => console.log('Table created successfully'),
```

171

```
      (error)                    =>
console.log('Error  creating  table:
', error)
        );
      });
    }, []);

    const saveData = () => {
      // Insert data into the table
      db.transaction((tx) => {
        tx.executeSql(
          'INSERT  INTO  users  (name)
VALUES (?)',
          ['John Doe'],
          ()    =>    console.log('Data
saved successfully'),
          (error)                    =>
console.log('Error  saving  data:  ',
error)
        );
      });
    };

    const fetchData = () => {
      // Retrieve data from the table
      db.transaction((tx) => {
        tx.executeSql(
          'SELECT * FROM users',
          [],
```

```
(tx, results) => {
    const         rows        =
results.rows.raw();
        console.log('Data
retrieved:', rows);
    },
    (error)                    =>
console.log('Error fetching data: ',
error)
    );
  });
};


return (
  <View>
    <Button   title="Save   Data"
onPress={saveData} />
    <Button   title="Fetch   Data"
onPress={fetchData} />
  </View>
  );
};


export default App;
```

o **Explanation**:

  ▪ We open the SQLite database and create
    a table called `users` with an `id` and
    `name` field.

173

- The `saveData` function inserts a new user into the table.
- The `fetchData` function retrieves all records from the `users` table.

  o SQLite is useful for relational data and provides advanced querying capabilities, like joins and filtering.

2. **Using Realm**: Realm is a more modern and flexible database that works for both simple and complex data. It is a mobile-first database that is optimized for performance, especially in mobile applications.

   o **Installing Realm**:

```bash
npm install realm
```

   o **Example (Using Realm)**:

```javascript
import React, { useEffect, useState } from 'react';
import { View, Text, Button } from 'react-native';
import Realm from 'realm';

const App = () => {
```

```
const [users, setUsers] =
useState([]);

  useEffect(() => {
    const initRealm = async () => {
      const realm = await
Realm.open({
        path: 'myrealm',
        schema: [{ name: 'User',
properties: { name: 'string' } }],
      });

      // Add a new user
      realm.write(() => {
        realm.create('User', { name:
'John Doe' });
      });

      // Retrieve users
      const users =
realm.objects('User');
      setUsers(users);
    };

    initRealm();
  }, []);

  return (
    <View>
```

175

```
{users.map((user, index) => (
    <Text
key={index}>{user.name}</Text>
    )))}
    <Button    title="Add    User"
onPress={() => {}} />
    </View>
  );
};

export default App;
```

o **Explanation**:

- **Realm** is opened with a schema for the `User` model.

- A user is created and saved to the Realm database.

- All users are retrieved and displayed on the screen.

o Realm simplifies the process of working with local databases and supports more complex operations, such as real-time data syncing, relationships between objects, and migrations.

Real-World Example: Saving User Preferences

Let's use **AsyncStorage** to save and load user preferences in a simple app. This could be useful for storing settings like the user's theme choice or language preference.

1. **Saving User Preferences**:

```javascript
import React, { useState, useEffect } from 'react';
import { View, Text, Button } from 'react-native';
import AsyncStorage from '@react-native-async-storage/async-storage';

const App = () => {
  const [theme, setTheme] = useState('light');

  // Save theme preference
  const saveTheme = async (theme) => {
    try {
      await AsyncStorage.setItem('@user_theme', theme);
      setTheme(theme);
    } catch (error) {
```

```
        console.log('Error saving theme: ',
error);
    }
  };

  // Load theme preference
  const loadTheme = async () => {
    try {
      const    storedTheme    =    await
AsyncStorage.getItem('@user_theme');
      if (storedTheme) {
        setTheme(storedTheme);
      }
    } catch (error) {
      console.log('Error loading theme: ',
error);
    }
  };

  useEffect(() => {
    loadTheme(); // Load theme on app load
  }, []);

  return (
    <View>
      <Text>Current Theme: {theme}</Text>
      <Button title="Switch to Dark Theme"
onPress={() => saveTheme('dark')} />
```

```
      <Button    title="Switch    to    Light
Theme"  onPress={()  =>  saveTheme('light')}
/>
    </View>
  );
};


export default App;
```

- o **Explanation**:
  - The `saveTheme` function stores the theme preference in AsyncStorage.
  - The `loadTheme` function retrieves the stored theme when the app is loaded and sets it to the `theme` state.

Conclusion

In this chapter, we explored how to manage local data in React Native using **AsyncStorage**, **SQLite**, and **Realm**. **AsyncStorage** is ideal for small, lightweight data storage, while **SQLite** and **Realm** are better suited for managing more complex or larger datasets, such as structured relational data. We also provided a real-world example of saving and loading user preferences, which can be adapted to various use cases in your app.

By understanding and implementing these local storage solutions, you can create applications that persist data efficiently, providing a better user experience by saving preferences and data locally.

CHAPTER 16

DEBUGGING REACT NATIVE APPS

Debugging is an essential skill for any developer, especially when building mobile apps. React Native provides various tools and techniques to help you debug your applications, including **Chrome Developer Tools**, **React Native Debugger**, and strategies for diagnosing **performance issues**. In this chapter, we will dive into these tools and explore how to use them effectively for debugging React Native apps.

Using Chrome Developer Tools for Debugging

The **Chrome Developer Tools** are commonly used for debugging JavaScript code in web applications, but you can also use them with React Native. React Native uses JavaScriptCore (the engine behind JavaScript execution on iOS), and when running in development mode, it enables debugging through Chrome.

1. **Enabling Debugging in React Native**: To enable remote debugging in React Native:

    o Start your React Native app in development mode using `npx react-native run-android` or `npx react-native run-ios`.

181

- o Open the developer menu on your device or simulator:
  - **Android**: Shake the device or press `Ctrl` + `M` (Windows/Linux) or `Cmd` + `M` (Mac) in the emulator.
  - **iOS**: Press `Cmd` + `D` in the simulator.
- o From the developer menu, select **"Debug JS Remotely"**. This will open a new tab in Chrome, where the JavaScript code from your app will be executed and can be debugged.

2. **Using Chrome Developer Tools**: Once remote debugging is enabled, you can use Chrome Developer Tools to inspect and debug your app:

  - o **Console**: Check logs, warnings, and errors from your JavaScript code. Use `console.log()` in your code to output values and check if they match your expectations.
  - o **Sources**: Set breakpoints in your JavaScript code. You can pause execution at specific lines to inspect variables and step through the code.
  - o **Network**: Inspect network requests made by your app. You can view the request details, including the headers, body, and responses, to identify issues with your API calls.
  - o **Elements**: Although this is more relevant for web apps, in React Native, you can use the "Elements"

tab to inspect the component tree and the styles applied to components.

3. **Example of Using Chrome Developer Tools**: Here's how you can use the console for debugging:

```javascript
const fetchData = async () => {
  try {
    const response = await fetch('https://jsonplaceholder.typicode.com/posts');
    const data = await response.json();
    console.log('Fetched Data:', data); // Log the data to the console
  } catch (error) {
    console.error('Error fetching data:', error); // Log any errors
  }
};
```

○ You can open the **Console** tab in Chrome Developer Tools to view the logged data.

Error Handling and Using React Native Debugger

Error handling is crucial for providing a seamless experience to users and for debugging your app during development. React Native provides various ways to handle and display errors, as well

183

as a dedicated **React Native Debugger** to make debugging more efficient.

1. **Using try/catch for Error Handling**: To handle asynchronous errors (e.g., when fetching data), you can use the `try/catch` block. This ensures that errors are caught and logged appropriately.

   Example:

   ```javascript
   const fetchData = async () => {
     try {
       const response = await fetch('https://jsonplaceholder.typicode.com/posts');
       const data = await response.json();
       console.log('Data fetched:', data);
     } catch (error) {
       console.error('Error fetching data:', error);
     }
   };
   ```

2. **Using React Native Debugger**: **React Native Debugger** is an all-in-one tool for debugging React Native apps. It combines **Redux DevTools**, **Chrome Developer Tools**, and **React DevTools** into one application.

- o **Installing React Native Debugger**: To install React Native Debugger, follow the steps on the official GitHub page.
  - Install via **Homebrew** on macOS:

    bash

    ```
    brew install --cask react-
    native-debugger
    ```

  - Alternatively, download the app directly from GitHub for your operating system.
- o **Using React Native Debugger**: Once you have installed **React Native Debugger**, open the app, and ensure it's connected to your React Native project:
  - Start your React Native app in development mode (`npx react-native run-android` or `npx react-native run-ios`).
  - From the developer menu, select **"Enable Debugging"** to connect to **React Native Debugger**.
  - React Native Debugger will show you logs, network requests, the Redux state (if you're using Redux), and more.

185

3. **Example**: Inspecting Redux State in React Native Debugger: If you're using Redux for state management, React Native Debugger shows the Redux state and actions. You can see the state changes, actions dispatched, and even time-travel to previous actions to debug your app's behavior.

Debugging Performance Issues

Performance issues, such as slow UI rendering, excessive CPU usage, or laggy animations, are common in mobile apps. React Native provides several tools and techniques to help diagnose and fix performance problems.

1. **Profiling with React DevTools**: React DevTools is a powerful tool for inspecting the component tree, understanding the rendering performance, and identifying unnecessary re-renders. To use React DevTools in React Native:

    o   Install **React DevTools** globally:

    ```bash

    npm install -g react-devtools
    ```

    o   Start React DevTools:

    ```bash
    ```

```
react-devtools
```

o   This will open a window where you can inspect the React component tree, view props and state, and see component performance metrics.

2. **Performance Monitor**: React Native provides a built-in **Performance Monitor** tool that displays key performance metrics, such as the frame rate, JS thread, and UI thread performance. To enable it:

   o   Open the developer menu and select **"Show Perf Monitor"**.

   o   This will display an overlay showing the performance of your app. Pay attention to **JS thread** and **UI thread** times. If the UI thread time exceeds 16ms, the app may experience jank or lag.

3. **Identifying Expensive Renders**: One common performance issue in React Native apps is unnecessary re-renders. You can optimize component rendering by using the following techniques:

   o   **React.memo**: This is a higher-order component that prevents unnecessary re-renders by memoizing the component's output.

```
javascript
```

```
const          MyComponent          =
React.memo((props) => {
   return <Text>{props.text}</Text>;
});
```

- o **PureComponent**: This is a base class for components that only re-render when props or state change.

4. **Tracking Memory Leaks**: Memory leaks can occur when components are not properly cleaned up, leading to an increase in memory usage over time. React Native's **useEffect** hook can be used to clean up resources when components unmount.

   Example (Cleaning up with useEffect):

   javascript

```
useEffect(() => {
  const interval = setInterval(() => {
    console.log('Interval running');
  }, 1000);

  // Cleanup on component unmount
  return () => clearInterval(interval);
}, []);
```

5. **Using Hermes for Improved Performance**: **Hermes** is a JavaScript engine optimized for React Native. Enabling

Hermes can significantly improve app startup time and reduce memory usage.

- o To enable Hermes, add the following to your `android/app/build.gradle` file:

```gradle

project.ext.react = [
  entryFile: file("index.js"),
  enableHermes: true
]
```

- o After enabling Hermes, rebuild your app to see the performance benefits.

Conclusion

In this chapter, we covered essential tools and techniques for debugging React Native apps:

- **Chrome Developer Tools** allow you to debug JavaScript and network requests with ease.
- **React Native Debugger** combines several tools, including Redux DevTools and React DevTools, to provide a comprehensive debugging experience.
- **Performance issues** can be identified and fixed using tools like the **Performance Monitor**, **React DevTools**,

and strategies to prevent unnecessary re-renders and memory leaks.

By using these debugging tools and performance optimization strategies, you can ensure your React Native apps run smoothly and provide an excellent user experience. Debugging is a vital skill, and mastering these tools will help you troubleshoot issues effectively and improve the overall quality of your app.

CHAPTER 17

TESTING REACT NATIVE APPS

Testing is a crucial part of the development process that helps ensure the reliability, stability, and performance of your React Native app. In this chapter, we will explore how to implement **unit testing**, **UI testing**, and **end-to-end (E2E) testing** using popular testing frameworks such as **Jest**, **Detox**, and **Appium**.

Unit Testing with Jest

Jest is the default testing framework for React Native and is used for unit testing JavaScript code. It allows you to test individual functions, components, or methods to ensure that they behave as expected. Jest comes with built-in test runners, assertion libraries, and mock functions.

1. **Setting Up Jest**: Jest comes preconfigured when you create a React Native project using **React Native CLI**. If you're using Expo, you can set it up by installing the necessary dependencies:

    bash

    ```
    npm install --save-dev jest @testing-
    library/react-native
    ```

In the project, Jest will automatically look for files with the `.test.js` or `.spec.js` extension.

2. **Writing Unit Tests with Jest**: Unit tests focus on testing individual units of logic. This can include testing functions, methods, or smaller parts of components.

Example (Testing a simple function):

```javascript
// math.js
export const add = (a, b) => a + b;
export const subtract = (a, b) => a - b;
```

```javascript
// math.test.js
import { add, subtract } from './math';

test('adds 1 + 2 to equal 3', () => {
  expect(add(1, 2)).toBe(3);
});

test('subtracts 2 - 1 to equal 1', () => {
  expect(subtract(2, 1)).toBe(1);
});
```

- o **Explanation**:
  - `test` is used to define a test case.

- expect is used to check the result and verify it with toBe.
- The above tests ensure that the add and subtract functions are working correctly.

3. **Mocking Dependencies**: Often, you need to test a function that depends on other modules or APIs. In Jest, you can use mocks to simulate these dependencies and isolate the function you're testing.

Example (Mocking a dependency):

javascript

```
// fetchData.js
export const fetchData = (url) => {
  return  fetch(url).then((response)  =>
response.json());
};


// fetchData.test.js
import { fetchData } from './fetchData';

jest.mock('fetch'); // Mock the fetch API

test('fetches data from an API', async ()
=> {
  const mockResponse = { data: 'sample
data' };
```

```
fetch.mockResolvedValueOnce({ json: ()
=> mockResponse });

const        data       =        await
fetchData('https://api.example.com/data')
;
  expect(data).toEqual(mockResponse);
});
```

o **Explanation**:

▪ `jest.mock()` is used to mock the `fetch` function.

▪ `mockResolvedValueOnce()` simulates a resolved value for `fetch`.

4. **Testing React Components**: React Native components can also be unit tested. The **React Testing Library** provides utilities for rendering components and interacting with them in tests.

Example (Testing a React Native component):

```javascript
javascript

// MyComponent.js
import React from 'react';
import { Text, Button, View } from 'react-
native';

const MyComponent = ({ onPress }) => (
```

```
  <View>
    <Button onPress={onPress} title="Press
Me" />
    <Text>Test</Text>
  </View>
);


export default MyComponent;
javascript

// MyComponent.test.js
import React from 'react';
import { render, fireEvent } from
'@testing-library/react-native';
import MyComponent from './MyComponent';

test('button press triggers the callback',
() => {
  const onPressMock = jest.fn();
  const { getByText } = render(<MyComponent
onPress={onPressMock} />);

  fireEvent.press(getByText('Press Me'));

expect(onPressMock).toHaveBeenCalledTimes
(1);
});
```

o **Explanation**:

195

- `render` is used to render the component.
- `fireEvent.press` simulates a button press.
- `jest.fn()` is used to create a mock function and check if it was called.

UI Testing with Detox

Detox is a popular tool for UI testing React Native applications. It allows you to simulate user interactions and validate the app's UI behavior on real devices or simulators/emulators. Detox provides end-to-end testing but focuses on testing the app's UI components.

1. **Setting Up Detox**: Install the Detox dependencies and configure it to work with your project:

bash

```
npm install --save-dev detox
npm install --save-dev detox-cli
```

2. **Configuring Detox**: Add Detox configurations to your `package.json` file:

json

```
"detox": {
  "configurations": {
```

```
"ios.sim.debug": {
    "binaryPath":
"ios/build/Build/Products/Debug-
iphonesimulator/myapp.app",
    "build":    "xcodebuild    -workspace
ios/myapp.xcworkspace    -scheme    myapp    -
configuration Debug -sdk iphonesimulator -
derivedDataPath ios/build",
    "type": "ios.simulator",
    "name": "iPhone 11"
    }
  }
}
```

3. **Writing Detox Tests**: Detox tests simulate user interactions with the app to test the UI.

   Example (Testing a Button Click):

   ```
   javascript
   ```

   ```javascript
   describe('MyApp', () => {
     beforeAll(async () => {
       await device.launchApp();
     });

     it('should display a button and respond
   to press', async () => {
       await    expect(element(by.text('Press
   Me'))).toBeVisible();
   ```

```
    await          element(by.text('Press
Me')).tap();
    await      expect(element(by.text('You
pressed the button!')))).toBeVisible();
  });
});
```

- o **Explanation**:
  - `beforeAll` launches the app before the tests run.
  - `expect` checks if the element (button) is visible.
  - `tap()` simulates a tap on the button, and the test verifies that the resulting UI change is correct.

End-to-End Testing with Appium

Appium is a cross-platform tool for automating mobile apps and testing them on real devices or simulators/emulators. It can be used for both **iOS** and **Android** and is suitable for automating user flows and validating app behavior end-to-end.

1. **Setting Up Appium**: Install Appium and its dependencies:

```
bash
```

```
npm install -g appium
```

2. **Creating an Appium Test**: Appium uses **WebDriver** to interact with the mobile app, and the tests are typically written in JavaScript or other supported languages. You need to write tests that simulate user interactions with your app, such as tapping buttons, entering text, and verifying the UI.

   Example (Appium Test for a Button Press):

```javascript
const { remote } = require('webdriverio');

let driver;

beforeAll(async () => {
  driver = await remote({
    capabilities: {
      platformName: 'iOS',
      platformVersion: '14.0',
      deviceName: 'iPhone 11',
      app: '/path/to/your/app',
      automationName: 'XCUITest',
    },
  });
});
```

```
afterAll(async () => {
  await driver.deleteSession();
});


it('should click on the button', async ()
=> {
  const button = await driver.$('~Press
Me'); // Locator for the button
  await button.click();
  const result = await driver.$('~You
pressed the button!');
  expect(await
result.isDisplayed()).toBe(true);
});
```

- o **Explanation**:
  - The test launches the app, taps on a button labeled "Press Me," and checks whether the text "You pressed the button!" appears after the action.
  - `driver.$` is used to locate elements by their accessibility labels or other selectors.

3. **Appium and Device Setup**: Appium requires you to set up a simulator or real device and configure the desired capabilities to test on a specific platform and device. The `platformName`, `deviceName`, and `app` capabilities specify the target device and app for testing.

Conclusion

In this chapter, we covered the essential techniques for **testing React Native apps**:

- **Unit testing with Jest** allows you to test individual functions and components in isolation.
- **UI testing with Detox** simulates user interactions with the app to verify the UI's behavior.
- **End-to-end testing with Appium** allows you to automate complete user flows, testing the app on real devices or simulators.

By integrating these testing frameworks into your development workflow, you can ensure that your React Native applications are reliable, maintainable, and free of regressions, providing a better user experience.

CHAPTER 18

PERFORMANCE OPTIMIZATION IN REACT NATIVE

As your React Native application grows, performance can become a critical issue, especially on lower-end devices. This chapter covers techniques and best practices for identifying performance bottlenecks and optimizing your React Native app. We will explore strategies such as **memory management**, **rendering optimization with PureComponent and memoization**, and general tips for improving app performance.

Identifying and Optimizing Performance Bottlenecks

Before optimizing, it's crucial to identify where the performance bottlenecks are occurring. React Native provides several tools to help track down performance issues, including built-in **Performance Monitor** and **React DevTools**.

1. **Using the Performance Monitor**: React Native has a built-in **Performance Monitor** that displays key performance metrics in real-time. You can enable it from the developer menu.

     o Open the developer menu by pressing `Cmd + D` (iOS) or `Ctrl + M` (Android).

o Select **"Show Perf Monitor"**.

o The Performance Monitor shows:

- **FPS (Frames per second)**: Ideally, your app should run at 60 FPS to provide a smooth user experience. If it drops below 30 FPS, the app will appear laggy.

- **JS thread and UI thread times**: The JS thread handles JavaScript execution, and the UI thread manages rendering. If either thread is overloaded, the app may become unresponsive.

2. **Profiling with React DevTools**: React DevTools can be used to profile the component tree and identify unnecessary re-renders.

o **Why Re-Renders Matter**: Re-renders are expensive in React Native, especially if you have deeply nested components. Frequent unnecessary re-renders can slow down your app, especially with complex UI.

o **React DevTools** provides a "highlight updates" feature, which visually shows which components are being re-rendered when the state or props change. This can help you pinpoint excessive renders.

3. **Using the Chrome Developer Tools**: For deeper analysis, the **Chrome Developer Tools** can be used when you enable **Remote JS Debugging** in your app.

    o   The **Timeline** tab lets you inspect and profile your app's performance, showing where slow operations are happening, including JavaScript execution and UI updates.

4. **Performance Bottlenecks**: Common performance bottlenecks include:

    o   **Unnecessary re-renders**: Caused by changes in state or props that trigger a re-render, even if the component doesn't need to update.

    o   **Large Lists**: Rendering large lists of items can cause performance issues, particularly if the entire list is rendered at once.

    o   **Heavy computations**: Running heavy computations on the JS thread can block the UI thread, causing lag.

Tools to Identify Bottlenecks:

o   **React Native Performance Monitor**
o   **React DevTools**
o   **Flipper** (A platform for debugging iOS and Android apps, integrated with React Native)

Memory Management Tips

Managing memory is crucial for mobile apps, as improper memory usage can lead to crashes and degraded performance, especially on devices with limited resources.

1. **Reducing Memory Leaks**:
   - Memory leaks occur when objects or resources are not properly released after use, causing the app to consume more and more memory over time. Common causes include:
     - **Event listeners not being removed**.
     - **Timers or intervals not being cleared**.
     - **Unnecessary references to components or objects**.

   Example (Cleaning Up Resources):

   javascript

   ```
   useEffect(() => {
     const intervalId = setInterval(() => {
       console.log('This runs every second');
     }, 1000);

     // Cleanup when the component is
   unmounted
     return () => clearInterval(intervalId);
   ```

```
},  []);
```

- o In the example above, `clearInterval()` is used to stop the interval when the component unmounts, preventing a memory leak.

2. **Use Weak References for Objects**: JavaScript provides the **WeakMap** and **WeakSet** structures, which hold weak references to objects, meaning the garbage collector can clean them up when they are no longer referenced. This can be useful when working with large datasets or objects that are not always needed.

3. **Optimizing Image Assets**: Large images can quickly consume a significant amount of memory, leading to app crashes or sluggish performance. You should:
   - o Use **image compression** tools to reduce the file size of images.
   - o Use **image caching** to avoid reloading the same image multiple times.
   - o Utilize **lazy loading** for images, especially when displaying large lists or grids.

4. **Avoiding Memory Leaks in Event Listeners**: When adding event listeners or subscriptions, always ensure that they are properly removed when no longer needed. This can be done with cleanup functions in **useEffect** or by manually removing event listeners.

Improving Rendering Speed with PureComponent and Memoization

Rendering optimization is critical for React Native apps, particularly when you are working with large datasets or complex components. There are two key techniques for improving rendering speed: using **PureComponent** and **memoization**.

1. **Using PureComponent**: **PureComponent** is a built-in React component that implements `shouldComponentUpdate()` for you. It compares the current props and state with the previous ones and only re-renders the component if there is a change. This reduces unnecessary re-renders and improves performance.

   PureComponent Example:

   ```javascript
   import React, { PureComponent } from 'react';
   import { Text, View } from 'react-native';

   class MyComponent extends PureComponent {
     render() {
       return (
         <View>
   ```

```
        <Text>{this.props.text}</Text>
      </View>
    );
  }
}
```

- o In this example, `MyComponent` extends `PureComponent`, and it will only re-render if the `text` prop changes. If `text` stays the same, React Native skips the render and improves performance.

2. **Memoization with React.memo**: **React.memo** is a higher-order component that memoizes a functional component. It prevents unnecessary re-renders by comparing the current props with the previous ones.

   React.memo Example:

```javascript
import React from 'react';
import { Text, View } from 'react-native';

const MyComponent = React.memo(({ text })
=> {
  return (
    <View>
      <Text>{text}</Text>
    </View>
```

```
    );
});
```

```
export default MyComponent;
```

- o In this example, `React.memo` wraps `MyComponent`, which ensures that the component only re-renders when the `text` prop changes.

3. **Memoization of Functions (useCallback and useMemo)**:
   - o **useCallback** and **useMemo** are hooks that memoize functions and values, respectively, preventing unnecessary recalculations and function recreations.

useCallback Example:

```
javascript
```

```javascript
import React, { useState, useCallback }
from 'react';
import { Button } from 'react-native';

const MyComponent = () => {
  const [count, setCount] = useState(0);

  const increment = useCallback(() => {
    setCount(count + 1);
```

```
}, [count]);

  return    <Button    title="Increment"
onPress={increment} />;
};
```

- o **useCallback** memoizes the increment function, ensuring it is not recreated on every render, which can improve performance when passed down to child components.

useMemo Example:

```
javascript
```

```
import React, { useMemo, useState } from
'react';
import { Text, View } from 'react-native';

const MyComponent = () => {
  const [count, setCount] = useState(0);

  const doubledCount = useMemo(() => count
* 2, [count]);

  return (
    <View>
      <Text>Count: {count}</Text>
```

210

```
<Text>Doubled                     Count:
{doubledCount}</Text>
   </View>
  );
};
```

- o **useMemo** memoizes the result of the calculation (count * 2) and only recalculates it when count changes, improving performance when the calculation is expensive.

Additional Tips for Performance Optimization

1. **Avoid Inline Functions**: Inline functions (like those in JSX) can cause re-renders, as they create a new function on every render. Try to define functions outside the render cycle or use useCallback to memoize them.

2. **Use FlatList for Large Lists**: When rendering large lists of data, always use **FlatList** instead of **ScrollView**. FlatList only renders the items that are currently visible on the screen, reducing memory usage and improving performance.

Example (Using FlatList):

javascript

```
import React from 'react';
```

211

```
import { FlatList, Text } from 'react-
native';

const data = [...Array(1000).keys()]; //
Large data set

const App = () => {
  return (
    <FlatList
      data={data}
      renderItem={({    item    })    =>
<Text>{item}</Text>}
      keyExtractor={(item)             =>
item.toString()}
    />
  );
};

export default App;
```

3. **Optimize Animations**: Use **Animated API** for smoother animations and consider using **NativeDriver** for offloading animations to the native thread, improving performance.

4. **Use Image Caching**: Use libraries like **react-native-fast-image** for caching images and improving performance when loading remote images.

Conclusion

In this chapter, we covered performance optimization strategies for React Native apps:

- **Identifying and optimizing performance bottlenecks** using the Performance Monitor, React DevTools, and Chrome Developer Tools.
- **Memory management tips** to avoid memory leaks and optimize memory usage.
- **Improving rendering speed** with `PureComponent`, `React.memo`, and memoization techniques like `useCallback` and `useMemo`.

By applying these optimization techniques, you can significantly improve the performance of your React Native app, providing a smoother and more responsive user experience. Always profile your app and identify the areas that need optimization to ensure that your app runs efficiently on all devices.

CHAPTER 19

BUILDING A REAL-TIME CHAT APP

Real-time chat applications are among the most common types of apps users interact with daily. React Native, with its support for modern backend technologies, makes it easier than ever to build interactive and scalable real-time apps. In this chapter, we will walk through the process of building a **real-time chat app** using **Firebase** for messaging, **WebSockets** for real-time communication, and **push notifications** for user alerts.

Setting Up Firebase for Real-Time Messaging

Firebase is a powerful platform that provides various backend services, including real-time databases, authentication, and cloud functions. For a real-time chat app, we can leverage Firebase's **Firestore** (a NoSQL database) and **Firebase Authentication**.

1. **Setting Up Firebase in React Native**: First, you'll need to create a Firebase project and configure it in your React Native app.
   - o   Go to Firebase Console and create a new project.
   - o   Add an iOS/Android app to your Firebase project and follow the setup instructions.

    o   Install the necessary Firebase libraries:

```bash
npm        install        @react-native-
firebase/app            @react-native-
firebase/auth           @react-native-
firebase/firestore
```

2. **Configure Firebase**: For Android, modify your `android/build.gradle` and `android/app/build.gradle` to include Firebase dependencies (Firebase SDK, Firestore, etc.). You will also need to add your Firebase configuration file (google-services.json for Android or GoogleService-Info.plist for iOS).

3. **Firebase Authentication**: Firebase Authentication provides various authentication methods like email/password, Google sign-in, and more. For this example, we'll use email/password authentication.

Example (Setting up authentication):

```javascript
import    auth    from    '@react-native-
firebase/auth';

// Sign up user
```

```
const signUp = async (email, password) =>
{
  try {
    await
auth().createUserWithEmailAndPassword(ema
il, password);
  } catch (error) {
    console.log('Error  signing  up:  ',
error);
  }
};


// Sign in user
const signIn = async (email, password) =>
{
  try {
    await
auth().signInWithEmailAndPassword(email,
password);
  } catch (error) {
    console.log('Error  signing  in:  ',
error);
  }
};
```

4. **Setting Up Firestore for Real-Time Messaging**: Firestore allows us to store chat messages and listen for changes in real-time.

Example (Saving and Fetching Messages from Firestore):

```javascript
import firestore from '@react-native-firebase/firestore';

// Sending a message
const sendMessage = async (message, userId) => {
  try {
    await firestore().collection('messages').add({
      userId: userId,
      text: message,
      timestamp: firestore.FieldValue.serverTimestamp(),
    });
  } catch (error) {
    console.log('Error sending message: ', error);
  }
};

// Fetching messages in real-time
const fetchMessages = async () => {
  firestore()
    .collection('messages')
    .orderBy('timestamp', 'desc')
    .onSnapshot((querySnapshot) => {
```

217

```
      const          messages          =
querySnapshot.docs.map((doc)              =>
doc.data());
        console.log('Fetched   Messages:   ',
messages);
    });
};
```

- o In this example:
  - ▪ `sendMessage` stores a new message in the Firestore `messages` collection with a `timestamp`.
  - ▪ `fetchMessages` listens for updates to the `messages` collection in real-time, automatically fetching new messages as they are added.

5. **Display Messages**: You can use **FlatList** to display the list of messages in the chat UI.

Example (Rendering messages in the chat UI):

```javascript
import React, { useState, useEffect } from
'react';
import { FlatList, Text, View, TextInput,
Button } from 'react-native';

const ChatScreen = () => {
```

```
const     [messages,    setMessages]     =
useState([]);
  const   [newMessage,   setNewMessage]   =
useState('');

  useEffect(() => {
    const unsubscribe = fetchMessages();
    return () => unsubscribe();  // Cleanup
listener on unmount
  }, []);

  return (
    <View>
      <FlatList
        data={messages}
        renderItem={({    item    })    =>
<Text>{item.text}</Text>}
        keyExtractor={(item,   index)   =>
index.toString()}
      />
      <TextInput
        value={newMessage}
        onChangeText={(text)            =>
setNewMessage(text)}
      />
      <Button title="Send" onPress={() =>
sendMessage(newMessage, 'userId')} />
    </View>
  );
```

```
};
```

```
export default ChatScreen;
```

- o This setup renders chat messages in a `FlatList` and includes a text input field to compose new messages.

Building Chat Functionality with WebSockets

WebSockets provide a full-duplex communication channel that is ideal for real-time messaging. While Firebase provides a simple real-time solution, WebSockets offer more control and can be used to build a custom chat server.

1. **Setting Up WebSocket Server**:
   - o You can use a Node.js server with **socket.io** to handle real-time communication. First, install `socket.io`:

   bash

   ```
   npm install socket.io
   ```

   - o Here's a basic setup for a WebSocket server using **socket.io**:

   javascript

```
const              io           =
require('socket.io')(server);    //
server is an HTTP server

io.on('connection', (socket) => {
  console.log('a user connected');
  socket.on('disconnect', () => {
    console.log('user
disconnected');
  });

  socket.on('chatMessage', (message)
=> {
    io.emit('chatMessage', message);
// Broadcast message to all clients
  });
});
```

2. **Setting Up WebSocket in React Native**: You can use the `socket.io-client` library to connect your React Native app to the WebSocket server.

Install `socket.io-client`:

```bash
bash
```

```
npm install socket.io-client
```

221

Example (Connecting and Sending/Receiving Messages with WebSocket):

javascript

```javascript
import io from 'socket.io-client';
import React, { useState, useEffect } from 'react';
import { TextInput, Button, View, Text } from 'react-native';

const socket = io('http://localhost:3000');   // Connect to WebSocket server

const ChatScreen = () => {
  const [message, setMessage] = useState('');
  const [messages, setMessages] = useState([]);

  useEffect(() => {
    socket.on('chatMessage', (msg) => {
      setMessages((prevMessages) => [...prevMessages, msg]);
    });

    return () => socket.off('chatMessage');
```

```
}, []);

const sendMessage = () => {
  socket.emit('chatMessage', message);
  setMessage('');
};

return (
  <View>
    {messages.map((msg, index) => (
      <Text key={index}>{msg}</Text>
    ))}
    <TextInput
      value={message}
      onChangeText={setMessage}
      placeholder="Type a message"
    />
    <Button              title="Send"
onPress={sendMessage} />
  </View>
);
};

export default ChatScreen;
```

o This example connects to a WebSocket server,
   listens for incoming messages with
   `socket.on('chatMessage')`, and sends

messages   with
`socket.emit('chatMessage').`

Integrating Push Notifications

Push notifications are essential for real-time apps, especially for keeping users engaged and informed when they're not actively using the app.

1. **Setting Up Firebase Cloud Messaging (FCM)**: Firebase Cloud Messaging (FCM) allows you to send push notifications to your React Native app. Follow these steps to set up FCM in your Firebase project:
   - o Go to Firebase Console, select your project, and navigate to **Cloud Messaging** under **Project settings**.
   - o Enable FCM and download the `google-services.json` or `GoogleService-Info.plist` for Android or iOS, respectively.

2. **Installing Firebase Cloud Messaging in React Native**: Install the required FCM libraries:

```bash
npm install @react-native-firebase/messaging
```

3. **Requesting Permissions for Push Notifications**: You need to request notification permissions on iOS (Android permissions are handled automatically).

Example (Requesting Permissions):

```javascript
import messaging from '@react-native-firebase/messaging';

const requestPermission = async () => {
  const authStatus = await messaging().requestPermission();
  const enabled =
    authStatus === messaging.AuthorizationStatus.AUTHORIZED ||
    authStatus === messaging.AuthorizationStatus.PROVISIONAL;
  if (enabled) {
    console.log('Notification permission granted');
  } else {
    console.log('Notification permission denied');
  }
};
```

4. **Receiving Push Notifications**: Set up listeners to handle incoming push notifications:

Example (Handling Notifications):

javascript

```javascript
import messaging from '@react-native-firebase/messaging';

useEffect(() => {
  // Foreground notifications
  const unsubscribeOnMessage = messaging().onMessage(async (remoteMessage) => {
    console.log('Foreground notification received: ', remoteMessage);
  });

  // Background notifications
  const unsubscribeOnNotificationOpenedApp = messaging().onNotificationOpenedApp(
    (remoteMessage) => {
      console.log('Notification caused app to open: ', remoteMessage);
    }
  );

  // App is opened from a terminated state
```

226

```
messaging()
  .getInitialNotification()
  .then((remoteMessage) => {
    if (remoteMessage) {
        console.log('App   opened   from   a
notification:', remoteMessage);
    }
  });

  return () => {
    unsubscribeOnMessage();
    unsubscribeOnNotificationOpenedApp();
  };
}, []);
```

o This code sets up listeners for foreground and background notifications and handles app launch from a terminated state due to a notification.

Conclusion

In this chapter, we learned how to build a **real-time chat app** using **Firebase** for real-time messaging, **WebSockets** for full-duplex communication, and **push notifications** to keep users engaged.

- Firebase provides an easy-to-use platform for storing chat messages and authenticating users.

227

- WebSockets allow real-time communication with more flexibility and control over the server-side logic.
- Push notifications are essential for alerting users about new messages or events, even when they're not actively using the app.

By combining these technologies, you can create a robust and scalable real-time chat app that meets the needs of modern mobile users.

CHAPTER 20

HANDLING BACKGROUND TASKS AND NOTIFICATIONS

In modern mobile applications, background tasks and notifications are crucial features that enhance user engagement and improve functionality. React Native provides several solutions for handling background tasks and notifications, allowing developers to build apps that can execute tasks even when the app is in the background or closed. In this chapter, we will explore how to handle background tasks, manage notifications, and implement them in a real-world example: a to-do list app with notifications.

Working with Background Tasks in React Native

Background tasks are operations that run behind the scenes, often without direct user interaction. These tasks can include activities like syncing data, checking for new messages, or updating location information. React Native provides several libraries and APIs to handle background tasks.

1. **Using `react-native-background-fetch`**: One of the most popular libraries for handling background tasks in React Native is **react-native-background-fetch**. This

library allows you to execute tasks even when the app is in the background or terminated.

Installation:

```bash
npm install @transistorsoft/react-native-
background-fetch
```

Basic Setup:

- o   For iOS, make sure you configure background fetch in your Xcode project by enabling the background fetch capability.
- o   For Android, ensure you have the correct permissions and set up the necessary configuration in the `AndroidManifest.xml`.

Example (Setting up Background Fetch):

```javascript
import        BackgroundFetch        from
'@transistorsoft/react-native-background-
fetch';

const configureBackgroundTask = async () =>
{
```

```
const onBackgroundFetchEvent = async
(taskId) => {
    console.log('[BackgroundFetch]
taskId:', taskId);

    // Simulate a background task
    // For example, sync data with a server
or fetch new messages
    try {
        // Perform background task
        console.log('Running        background
task...');

        // Make sure to finish the task when
done
        BackgroundFetch.finish(taskId);
    } catch (error) {
        console.error('Error   in   background
task:', error);
        BackgroundFetch.finish(taskId);   //
Finish with error if task fails
    }
};

    // Configure background fetch
    BackgroundFetch.configure(
    {
        minimumFetchInterval: 15,  // Fetch
every 15 minutes
```

```
      stopOnTerminate: false,   // Continue
fetching after app is terminated
      startOnBoot: true,          // Start
fetch after device reboot
    },
    onBackgroundFetchEvent, // Background
fetch callback
    (error) => {
      console.error('Background        fetch
failed:', error);
    }
  );
};


useEffect(() => {
  configureBackgroundTask();

  return () => {
    // Clean up on unmount
    BackgroundFetch.stop();
  };
}, []);
```

- o **Explanation**:
    - ▪ `BackgroundFetch.configure` sets up the background task, specifying the interval at which tasks should run (`minimumFetchInterval`) and

whether the task should stop when the app is terminated.

- `BackgroundFetch.finish(taskId )` is used to indicate that the background task has been completed.

2. **Scheduling Background Tasks**: Background tasks can be scheduled to run periodically, as shown above. If you need tasks to run at a specific time or in response to specific events (like location updates), you can customize the behavior of the background task by adding appropriate triggers.

Using Libraries for Local Notifications

Local notifications are an essential part of mobile apps, alerting users to important events or updates even when the app is not actively in use. React Native provides libraries like **react-native-push-notification** to handle local notifications efficiently.

1. **Setting Up `react-native-push-notification`:** **react-native-push-notification** is a popular library that provides a simple interface for local notifications.

   Installation:

   ```bash
   npm install react-native-push-notification
   ```

Configuration:

- o For iOS, ensure that you request permission to display notifications in the app, and configure the necessary settings in the **Info.plist**.
- o For Android, update the **AndroidManifest.xml** to include the necessary permissions and configuration for push notifications.

Example (Setting Up Local Notifications):

```javascript

import PushNotification from 'react-native-push-notification';

// Configure push notifications
PushNotification.configure({
  onNotification: function (notification) {
    console.log('Notification received:', notification);
  },
  requestPermissions: Platform.OS === 'ios',
});

// Scheduling a local notification
const scheduleNotification = () => {
```

234

```
PushNotification.localNotificationSchedul
e({
    message: 'This is your reminder to
complete a task!',
    date: new Date(Date.now() + 5 * 1000),
// Schedule for 5 seconds later
  });
};
```

- o **Explanation**:
  - PushNotification.localNotific ationSchedule allows you to schedule notifications that will be delivered at a specified time. In this example, a notification is scheduled to be delivered 5 seconds after the function is called.

2. **Handling Notifications**: Notifications can be handled through the onNotification callback, where you can execute specific actions when a notification is received, such as updating the UI or navigating to a specific screen.

Real-World Example: Building a To-Do List App with Notifications

Let's combine **background tasks** and **local notifications** to build a simple **To-Do List App**. In this app, users can set tasks with reminders, and the app will notify them when the task is due.

1. **App Setup**:
   o The user will be able to add tasks, set a due time for each task, and receive a notification when the task is due.

   App Example:

```javascript
import React, { useState, useEffect } from 'react';
import { View, Text, TextInput, Button, FlatList } from 'react-native';
import PushNotification from 'react-native-push-notification';
import BackgroundFetch from '@transistorsoft/react-native-background-fetch';

const App = () => {
  const [task, setTask] = useState('');
  const [tasks, setTasks] = useState([]);
  const [dueTime, setDueTime] = useState('');

  // Function to add a new task
  const addTask = () => {
    const newTask = {
      id: tasks.length + 1,
```

```
    task: task,
    dueTime: dueTime,
  };
  setTasks([...tasks, newTask]);

  // Schedule notification
  const dueDate = new Date(dueTime);

PushNotification.localNotificationSchedul
e({
    message: `Task Reminder: ${task}`,
    date: dueDate,
  });

  setTask('');
  setDueTime('');
};

// Function to configure background tasks
const configureBackgroundTask = async ()
=> {
  const onBackgroundFetchEvent = async
(taskId) => {
    console.log('[BackgroundFetch]
taskId:', taskId);
    // You can implement any background
sync logic here, like checking if the task
is due
    BackgroundFetch.finish(taskId);
```

```
    };

    BackgroundFetch.configure(
      {
        minimumFetchInterval: 15, // Every
15 minutes
        stopOnTerminate:   false,        //
Continue fetching when app is terminated
        startOnBoot: true,        // Start
fetching after device restart
      },
      onBackgroundFetchEvent,
      (error) => {
        console.log('Background        fetch
failed:', error);
      }
    );
  };

  useEffect(() => {
    configureBackgroundTask();

    return () => {
      BackgroundFetch.stop();
    };
  }, []);

  return (
    <View>
```

```
    <TextInput
      placeholder="Enter task"
      value={task}
      onChangeText={(text)                =>
setTask(text)}
    />
    <TextInput
      placeholder="Enter due time (e.g.,
2023-04-23T14:30:00)"
      value={dueTime}
      onChangeText={(text)                =>
setDueTime(text)}
    />
    <Button        title="Add        Task"
onPress={addTask} />
    <FlatList
      data={tasks}
      renderItem={({ item }) => (
        <View>
          <Text>{item.task}</Text>
          <Text>Due:
{item.dueTime}</Text>
        </View>
      )}
      keyExtractor={(item)                =>
item.id.toString()}
    />
  </View>
);
```

```
};
```

```
export default App;
```

- o **Explanation**:
  - The app allows users to add tasks with a due time, and the task will trigger a notification when the due time arrives.
  - **PushNotification.localNotificationSchedule** is used to schedule the notification at the specified time.
  - **Background tasks** are configured using `react-native-background-fetch` to perform periodic background checks (e.g., syncing tasks or checking reminders).
  - **FlatList** is used to display the list of tasks.

Conclusion

In this chapter, we covered the essentials of **handling background tasks** and **notifications** in React Native:

- We explored **background tasks** using `react-native-background-fetch`, allowing your app to execute tasks even when the app is not active.

- We implemented **local notifications** using **react-native-push-notification**, enabling us to alert users about important events like task reminders.
- Finally, we built a real-world **To-Do List App** where users can set tasks with notifications, making the app interactive and responsive.

By using these techniques, you can enhance your React Native apps with powerful background task management and push notifications, providing a richer and more engaging user experience.

CHAPTER 21

PREPARING YOUR APP FOR PRODUCTION

Once your React Native app is fully developed and tested, it's time to prepare it for production. Preparing your app involves generating necessary assets (like **app icons** and **splash screens**), configuring build settings for both **iOS** and **Android**, and ensuring that your app meets the **App Store** and **Google Play** guidelines. This chapter will walk you through each of these steps to get your app ready for release.

Generating App Icons and Splash Screens

App icons and splash screens are critical for user experience as they are the first things users see when opening your app. It's essential to ensure they are high-quality and appropriately sized for all devices.

1. **App Icons**: App icons are used in multiple places, including the home screen, app drawer, and task switcher. You need to generate different sizes of your icon for iOS and Android.

   o **iOS App Icons**: iOS requires multiple sizes of app icons. These sizes are defined in the Xcode project, and you must provide them in your `Assets.xcassets` directory.

- You can use tools like **Image Asset Generator** to create all the required icon sizes.

- Use **Xcode** to set the app icon in your iOS project. After creating the necessary sizes, you can drag them into the `AppIcon` section of the **Assets** catalog in Xcode.

o **Android App Icons**: Android requires icons in multiple sizes, including **ldpi**, **mdpi**, **hdpi**, **xhdpi**, **xxhdpi**, and **xxxhdpi**.

- You can use tools like **Image Asset Studio** in Android Studio to generate the necessary icon sizes.

- In **Android Studio**, navigate to **File > New > Image Asset** to create your app icon and set it for different screen densities.

o **Tools for Generating Icons**:

- **React Native Asset Generator**: This tool generates app icons and splash screens in all necessary sizes.

- **App Icon Generator**: Online tools that automatically generate all required sizes for iOS and Android.

Example (Using `react-native-make` for generating assets):

```bash
npx react-native set-icon --path ./assets/icon.png
```

2. **Splash Screens**: Splash screens are shown when the app is launched, usually for a few seconds, and are meant to provide an initial branding experience.
   o **iOS Splash Screens**: iOS uses a **launch storyboard** to display splash screens. You can create a static splash screen using a **LaunchScreen.storyboard** in Xcode. Ensure the splash screen uses the same theme as your app and is styled accordingly.
     - **LaunchScreen.storyboard** in Xcode can be configured with different images or static content.
   o **Android Splash Screens**: Android uses a **launch theme** that's set in the `styles.xml` file. You should define a splash screen background color and image here.

244

- You can set the **android:windowBackground** property in the `styles.xml` to define the splash screen.
- For animated splash screens, use **React Native Splash Screen** library.

Example (Adding Splash Screen in `styles.xml` for Android):

xml

```
<style            name="LaunchTheme"
parent="Theme.AppCompat.Light.NoActionBar
">
  <item
name="android:windowBackground">@drawable
/splash_screen</item>
</style>
```

Example (Using `react-native-splash-screen` for splash screens):

bash

```
npm install react-native-splash-screen
```

- o In `App.js`, add:

```javascript
import SplashScreen from 'react-native-splash-screen';

useEffect(() => {
  SplashScreen.hide();    // Hide splash screen after app is ready
}, []);
```

Configuring Build Settings for iOS and Android

Once the assets are ready, the next step is configuring the build settings for both **iOS** and **Android** to ensure your app runs smoothly in production.

1. **Configuring iOS Build Settings**:
   - **Xcode Configuration**: Open your project in Xcode and configure the following:
     - **Bundle Identifier**: A unique identifier for your app (e.g., `com.yourcompany.appname`).
     - **Versioning**: Set the version number and build number. The version number corresponds to the app's version for users, and the build number represents an internal version of the app.
     - **Provisioning Profile**: Ensure you've set up a valid provisioning profile for

246

signing your app for release. You can configure this in the **Apple Developer Console**.

o **App Signing**: In Xcode, go to **Targets > YourApp > Signing & Capabilities** and select the appropriate team and provisioning profile for your app.

o **Optimizing App for Release**:

▪ In **Xcode**, set the build configuration to **Release** mode to ensure optimization.

▪ Enable **App Thinning** and **Bitcode** for better performance and smaller app size.

Example (Setting Version and Build Number in Info.plist):

xml

```
<key>CFBundleShortVersionString</key>
<string>1.0.0</string> <!-- App version -->
<key>CFBundleVersion</key>
<string>100</string> <!-- Build number -->
```

2. **Configuring Android Build Settings**:

o **AndroidManifest.xml**: Set the version code and version name in your AndroidManifest.xml file. The versionCode is an integer that is incremented with each new release, and `versionName` is the human-readable version string.

Example (Setting Version in `build.gradle` for Android):

gradle

```
android {
  defaultConfig {
    versionCode 1
    versionName "1.0.0"
  }
}
```

- o **App Signing**: To prepare your app for release, you must sign it with a private key. You can configure signing in the `android/gradle.properties` file and **signingConfigs** in the `build.gradle` file.

Example (Signing Config in `build.gradle`):

gradle

```
android {
  signingConfigs {
    release {
```

```
        storeFile
file("path/to/your.keystore")
        storePassword "your-store-password"
        keyAlias "your-key-alias"
        keyPassword "your-key-password"
    }
  }
  buildTypes {
    release {
      signingConfig signingConfigs.release
    }
  }
}
```

- o **Optimizing for Release**:
  - **Proguard**: Enable Proguard in `build.gradle` to shrink, obfuscate, and optimize your code for production.
  - **ShrinkResources**: Enable resource shrinking in `build.gradle` to reduce the app size by removing unused resources.

Example (Enabling Proguard and Shrinking Resources):

```
gradle

android {
  buildTypes {
```

```
release {
    minifyEnabled   true      // Enable
Proguard
    shrinkResources   true      // Shrink
unused resources
    proguardFiles
getDefaultProguardFile('proguard-android-
optimize.txt'), 'proguard-rules.pro'
    }
  }
}
```

Optimizing for App Store Guidelines

1. **App Store Guidelines**: To ensure your app is accepted by the **Apple App Store** or **Google Play Store**, it's important to adhere to their respective guidelines:

    o   **App Store (iOS)**:

        ▪   Ensure you have appropriate **privacy policies**, **terms of service**, and **permissions** (such as camera, location, etc.).

        ▪   Your app must not crash, freeze, or behave unpredictably.

        ▪   Make sure to include a clear and functional **app icon** and **splash screen**.

    o   **Google Play Store (Android)**:

- Google Play also requires a clear **privacy policy**, especially if your app collects user data.
- Ensure that the app runs well on a variety of screen sizes and Android versions.
- Avoid using private APIs or services not approved by Google.

2. **App Store Optimization (ASO)**: Optimize your app's listing by providing the following:

   o **App name** and **description** that are clear and keyword-optimized.

   o High-quality **screenshots** and a **promotional video** to showcase your app's features.

   o A concise **update log** for each new release, explaining new features and fixes.

3. **Testing for Release**: Before submitting your app to the store, conduct thorough testing:

   o **Beta Testing**: Use **TestFlight** for iOS or **Google Play Console's Beta Testing** feature for Android to get feedback from real users.

   o **Crash Reporting**: Integrate crash reporting tools like **Sentry** or **Firebase Crashlytics** to monitor issues after release.

4. **App Icon and Splash Screen**: Ensure that your app's **icon** and **splash screen** meet the guidelines of the respective store:

- o For iOS, the app icon should be clear, simple, and fit within the required size ranges.
- o For Android, follow the design specifications in the Android Material Design guidelines for icons.

Conclusion

In this chapter, we covered the steps needed to prepare your React Native app for production:

- We learned how to generate **app icons** and **splash screens** for both iOS and Android using tools and manual configuration.
- We explored **build settings for iOS and Android**, ensuring that the app is properly signed, optimized, and ready for release.
- We discussed how to adhere to **App Store guidelines** and prepare your app for submission to both the **Apple App Store** and **Google Play Store**, including tips on **App Store Optimization (ASO)** and testing.

By following these steps, you'll be able to confidently prepare your React Native app for production and submit it to the app stores for global distribution.

CHAPTER 22

DEPLOYING APPS TO THE APP STORE AND GOOGLE PLAY

Deploying your React Native app to the **App Store** and **Google Play** is the final step in making your app available to users worldwide. This chapter will guide you through the steps for submitting your app to both platforms, preparing the necessary assets, and handling app updates and versioning.

Steps for Submitting to the App Store and Google Play

1. **Submitting to the App Store (iOS)**: Submitting your app to the App Store requires you to follow Apple's guidelines, fill in the necessary metadata, and pass through the app review process.

   Step 1: Prepare Your App for Submission:

   - Make sure your app is thoroughly tested and runs without issues.
   - Ensure that all the **required icons**, **splash screens**, and **metadata** (app name, description, keywords, etc.) are properly set up.

o   Ensure that the app is **signed** and ready for release (you've already configured this in Xcode).

Step 2: Create an App Store Connect Account:

o   To submit an app, you need an **Apple Developer account**. Sign up at the Apple Developer Program page.

o   Once you have an account, go to **App Store Connect** (https://appstoreconnect.apple.com) to manage your apps.

Step 3: Set Up Your App in App Store Connect:

o   Go to the **App Store Connect** dashboard and select **My Apps**.

o   Click the + button to add a new app. Fill out the app's details, such as:

- **App Name**: Choose a unique name for your app.

- **Primary Language**: Set the default language for your app.

- **Bundle ID**: Use the bundle ID you created in Xcode when configuring your app.

- **SKU**: This is a unique identifier for your app.

Step 4: Upload Your App Using Xcode:

- o Open your project in **Xcode** and select **Product > Archive** to create an archive of your app.
- o After archiving, Xcode will open the **Organizer** window. From here, click **Distribute App** and select **App Store Connect > Upload**.
- o Follow the prompts to upload your app to **App Store Connect**.

Step 5: Submit Your App for Review:

- o After uploading, go back to **App Store Connect**, fill out the required information about your app (privacy policy, category, etc.), and then click **Submit for Review**.
- o Apple's review process can take a few days, and they will either approve or reject your app based on their guidelines.

2. **Submitting to Google Play (Android)**: Submitting an app to Google Play is a slightly simpler process, but it still requires careful preparation to meet Google's guidelines.

Step 1: Prepare Your App for Submission:

- o Make sure your app is fully tested on various Android devices and that it performs well.

o Set up your **versioning** and ensure you've signed your APK or AAB file (Android App Bundle).

Step 2: Create a Google Play Developer Account:

o To submit an app to Google Play, you need a **Google Play Developer account**. You can create one at the Google Play Console for a one-time fee.

Step 3: Set Up Your App in the Google Play Console:

o Go to the **Google Play Console**, and click **Create Application**.
o Fill out the details for your app:
  - **Title**: The name of your app on Google Play.
  - **Description**: A brief description of your app's features and functionalities.
  - **Category**: Choose the appropriate category for your app.
  - **Content Rating**: Set the appropriate rating for your app.

Step 4: Upload Your APK or AAB:

o In the **Google Play Console**, navigate to **Release > Production** and click **Create Release**.

o Upload your signed APK or AAB file.

o Add release notes (what's new in this version).

Step 5: Submit Your App for Review:

o Once your app is uploaded and all the metadata is filled out, click **Save** and then **Review**.

o Google Play's review process usually takes a few hours or a day.

o After approval, your app will be available for download on the Google Play Store.

Preparing Assets (Screenshots, Descriptions, etc.)

When submitting your app, you will need to provide various assets and metadata for both the **App Store** and **Google Play Store**. These assets help your app stand out and provide users with an understanding of what your app does.

1. **App Icons**:
   o **iOS**: App icons should be 1024x1024 pixels.
   o **Android**: The icon should be adaptive, with a 512x512 px size.
2. **Screenshots**: Screenshots help showcase your app's features and user interface. Both platforms require you to upload screenshots that reflect the app's core functionality.

o **iOS**: You'll need screenshots for all device sizes (iPhone, iPad, and possibly Apple Watch).

o **Android**: You need screenshots for different screen sizes (phone, tablet, etc.).

Best Practices for Screenshots:

o Use high-quality images that clearly represent your app's UI and features.

o Include 5-10 screenshots that showcase the app's most important features.

o For **Google Play**, provide **16:9** screenshots, and for **App Store**, use **5.5-inch screen resolution** for iPhone.

3. **App Descriptions**:

o **Short Description (Google Play)**: This is the tagline that will appear above the full description. Keep it concise and to the point.

o **Full Description**: Provide a detailed description of your app's features, benefits, and any unique selling points. Make sure to include relevant keywords to help your app get discovered.

4. **Privacy Policy**: Both the App Store and Google Play require you to provide a **privacy policy** if your app collects any user data. This includes things like:

o Accessing the camera, location, or contacts.

o Using third-party services (e.g., Firebase, Google Analytics).

o Storing user data or personal information.

You can create a privacy policy using online generators or consult with a legal professional to create one tailored to your app.

Handling App Updates and Versioning

Once your app is live, you will need to manage updates and versioning for both platforms. Proper versioning ensures that users always have the latest features and fixes.

1. **Versioning in iOS (App Store)**:

   o **Version Number**: This is a string (e.g., 1.0.0) that indicates the public release of the app.

   o **Build Number**: This is an integer that identifies the version of the app submitted for review.

You can set both values in your **Xcode project** in the Info.plist file.

Example (Setting Versioning in Xcode):

xml

```
<key>CFBundleShortVersionString</key>
```

```
<string>1.0.0</string> <!-- Version Number
-->
<key>CFBundleVersion</key>
<string>100</string> <!-- Build Number -->
```

2. **Versioning in Android (Google Play):**
   o **Version Code:** An integer that represents the version of the app.
   o **Version Name:** A human-readable string (e.g., 1.0.0) that shows the app version to users.

Example (Setting Versioning in `build.gradle` for Android):

```gradle
gradle

android {
  defaultConfig {
    versionCode 2  // Increment this value
with each release
    versionName "1.1.0"  // Version number
for users
  }
}
```

3. **App Updates:**
   o **iOS:** After submitting the update to App Store Connect, Apple will review the new version.

Once approved, users can download it via the App Store.

o **Android**: For Google Play, you upload the updated APK/AAB, and after review, the new version becomes available for download via the Google Play Store.

Tip: When releasing an update, always increment the version code and version number to ensure users receive the new version. Be sure to test the update thoroughly before submitting.

Conclusion

In this chapter, we covered the essential steps to deploy your React Native app to both the **App Store** and **Google Play**. These steps included:

- **Submitting the app** to both stores, including setting up accounts and filling out metadata.
- **Preparing assets** like icons, screenshots, and descriptions to make your app appealing to users.
- **Managing updates and versioning** to keep your app up-to-date with the latest features and fixes.

By following these steps, you can ensure that your app reaches its target audience smoothly and complies with the requirements of both app stores. Proper deployment is key to the success of your app, so make sure to plan and execute this process carefully.

CHAPTER 23

KEEPING UP WITH THE REACT NATIVE ECOSYSTEM

React Native is a rapidly evolving framework, and to stay competitive, it's important to keep up with the latest trends, libraries, tools, and updates. The React Native ecosystem is vast, with a variety of third-party libraries, tools, and community resources that can help you build more efficient, scalable, and feature-rich apps. In this chapter, we will explore popular libraries and tools in the React Native ecosystem, strategies for staying updated with React Native releases, and community resources that provide learning and support.

Popular Libraries and Tools in the React Native Ecosystem

React Native has a thriving ecosystem, filled with libraries that help developers add functionality quickly without reinventing the wheel. Here are some of the most widely used libraries and tools:

1. **Navigation**:
    o **React Navigation**: One of the most popular and flexible navigation libraries for React Native. It supports stack, tab, and drawer navigation, and can be customized to fit your needs.

```
bash
```

```
npm install @react-navigation/native
```

- React Navigation provides an intuitive API and works well with both functional and class components.

o **React Native Navigation**: A performance-optimized navigation library developed by Wix. It provides a more native-like experience and is better suited for apps with complex navigation needs.

```
bash
```

```
npm install react-native-navigation
```

2. **State Management**:

   o **Redux**: A predictable state container for JavaScript apps, commonly used with React Native for managing global state. It allows for clear data flow and is well-suited for large applications.

```
bash
```

```
npm install redux react-redux
```

o **Recoil**: A state management library developed by Facebook. It provides a simpler and more flexible alternative to Redux, especially for apps that need to share state between deeply nested components.

```bash
npm install recoil
```

o **React Query**: For handling asynchronous data fetching and caching. React Query simplifies data fetching, caching, synchronization, and more in your app.

```bash
npm install react-query
```

3. **Networking**:

o **Axios**: A promise-based HTTP client for making requests. It's simple, flexible, and allows for intercepting requests and responses.

```bash
npm install axios
```

o **Apollo Client**: For working with GraphQL. Apollo Client provides tools to query, cache, and manage the state of GraphQL data in React Native.

bash

```
npm install @apollo/client
```

4. **UI Components and Styling**:

   o **React Native Paper**: A library of Material Design components for React Native. It provides high-quality components with built-in theming and accessibility.

   bash

   ```
   npm install react-native-paper
   ```

   o **NativeBase**: Another UI toolkit for building cross-platform applications. It offers pre-built components like buttons, headers, and cards.

   bash

   ```
   npm install native-base
   ```

   o **Styled Components**: A library for styling React Native components using tagged template literals. It allows for scoped, dynamic, and declarative styling.

```bash
```

```bash
npm install styled-components
```

5. **Forms and Validation**:

   o **Formik**: A popular form management library in React Native. Formik simplifies the process of building and handling forms, including validation and submission.

   ```bash
   ```

   ```bash
   npm install formik
   ```

   o **React Hook Form**: A lightweight alternative to Formik, it uses hooks to manage form state and validation.

   ```bash
   ```

   ```bash
   npm install react-hook-form
   ```

6. **Testing**:

   o **Jest**: The default testing framework for React Native, used for unit testing JavaScript code. Jest also integrates well with other libraries like Enzyme and React Testing Library.

   ```bash
   ```

267

```
npm install jest
```

o **Detox**: A gray-box end-to-end testing framework that is specifically designed for React Native applications. Detox allows you to test the full behavior of your app on real devices and simulators.

```
bash
```

```
npm install detox
```

7. **Performance Optimization**:

o **React Native Reanimated**: An animation library that provides more powerful and smoother animations by running animations on the UI thread, which helps avoid performance bottlenecks.

```
bash
```

```
npm install react-native-reanimated
```

o **React Native Fast Image**: A library to handle images more efficiently, providing caching and faster loading.

```
bash
```

268

```
npm install react-native-fast-image
```

8. **Push Notifications**:

   o **React Native Push Notification**: A library for handling local and push notifications on both iOS and Android.

   bash

   ```
   npm    install    react-native-push-
   notification
   ```

   o **Firebase Cloud Messaging**: Firebase offers a robust solution for push notifications. React Native integrates easily with Firebase to enable push notifications in your app.

9. **Database and Storage**:

   o **Realm**: A mobile-first database solution that is easy to set up and scale. Realm is highly performant and can be used for both local storage and data synchronization across devices.

   bash

   ```
   npm install realm
   ```

   o **SQLite**: A lightweight, relational database engine for mobile devices. React Native's `react-native-sqlite-storage` can be used to integrate SQLite with your app.

```
bash
```

```
npm    install    react-native-sqlite-
storage
```

Staying Updated with React Native Releases

React Native is actively maintained, with frequent updates that improve performance, fix bugs, and add new features. Keeping your project up-to-date is essential for maintaining compatibility with new iOS and Android versions and ensuring optimal performance.

1. **Official React Native Blog**: The official React Native blog is the best place to stay updated on new releases, breaking changes, and performance improvements. Each release comes with detailed changelogs and migration guides.

2. **GitHub Repository**: The React Native GitHub repository is where all the source code, issues, and pull requests are managed. Watching the repository or subscribing to notifications will alert you about new releases.

3. **React Native Twitter and Community**: Follow the official **React Native Twitter account** and join the **React Native Community** on platforms like **Slack**, **Discord**, or

Reddit. These communities often share tips, resources, and news about the latest updates.

4. **React Native Newsletter**: There are several newsletters that focus on React Native development, such as React Native Newsletter. These newsletters summarize recent changes, articles, and community events related to React Native.

5. **Upgrading React Native**: When upgrading to a new version of React Native, make sure to follow the official upgrade guide for the smoothest transition. You can also use tools like **React Native Upgrade Helper** (https://react-native-community.github.io/upgrade-helper/) to assist with upgrading your project.

    Example (Upgrading React Native):

    ```bash
    npx react-native upgrade
    ```

6. **Release Notes**: Always check the release notes whenever a new version of React Native is released. The release notes contain important information about deprecated APIs, breaking changes, and new features that could affect your app.

Community Resources for Learning and Support

1. **Official React Native Documentation**: The React Native documentation is the most comprehensive resource for learning how to use React Native. It covers everything from installation to advanced topics like performance optimization and custom native modules.

2. **React Native Community and Forums**:

   o **Stack Overflow**: A great resource for troubleshooting and finding answers to common React Native problems. Use the `react-native` tag to filter relevant questions.

   o **GitHub Discussions**: React Native's GitHub repository has a Discussions section where community members share ideas, issues, and solutions.

   o **Reddit**: Subreddits like r/reactnative are active with discussions, tips, and tutorials from other React Native developers.

3. **Tutorials and Courses**:

   o **YouTube**: There are many free React Native tutorials available on YouTube, ranging from beginner to advanced topics. Channels like **Academind** and **Traversy Media** offer excellent content.

   o **Udemy**: Udemy offers paid courses for learning React Native at all skill levels. Look for highly-rated courses such as "React Native - The Practical Guide" by Maximilian Schwarzmüller.

4. **Podcasts**:

   o **React Native Radio**: A popular podcast that covers a variety of topics related to React Native, including interviews with industry experts, best practices, and new features.

   o **React Native EU Podcast**: Another podcast focused on React Native, featuring insights from developers working in the React Native ecosystem.

5. **Meetups and Conferences**:

   o **React Native Meetups**: There are local React Native meetups in many cities around the world. Check Meetup.com for a group near you.

   o **React Native Conferences**: Events like **React Native EU**, **Chain React**, and **React Conf** are great places to network, learn from experts, and stay up-to-date with the latest in the React Native ecosystem.

6. **Books**:

   o **"Learning React Native" by Bonnie Eisenman**: A great introductory book that covers all the fundamental concepts in React Native.

o **"React Native in Action" by Nader Dabit**: A comprehensive guide to building production-ready apps with React Native.

o **"React Native Cookbook" by Dan Ward**: A hands-on book filled with practical examples of React Native development.

Conclusion

The React Native ecosystem is vast and constantly evolving, with new tools, libraries, and updates being released regularly. To stay competitive and create modern, high-quality apps, it's crucial to stay updated with the latest developments in the ecosystem. By using the tools and libraries mentioned in this chapter, staying informed through community resources, and actively participating in the React Native community, you can ensure that your skills and apps are always up to date.

CHAPTER 24

CONCLUSION AND NEXT STEPS

As you reach the end of this book, you've covered a lot of ground in your journey to becoming a proficient React Native developer. You've learned the ins and outs of React Native, from setting up your development environment to deploying your app on the App Store and Google Play. In this final chapter, we'll recap the key concepts you've learned, encourage you to continue your learning journey, and provide some ideas for future app projects to help you expand your skills further.

Recap of Key Concepts Covered in the Book

Throughout this book, we explored several important aspects of React Native development:

1. **Getting Started with React Native**:
   o We covered how to set up the development environment and create your first React Native project.
   o You learned the core components and concepts of React Native, such as JSX, state, props, and the component lifecycle.

2. **Building Real-World Applications**:

- o We walked through how to build real-world apps, like a **chat app** with Firebase, a **to-do list app**, and other practical projects.
- o You learned how to integrate key services like **Firebase** for real-time messaging, **WebSockets** for real-time communication, and **push notifications** to engage users.

3. **Optimizing Your App**:

- o We explored how to optimize your app's performance, from identifying and resolving performance bottlenecks to improving rendering speeds using tools like **PureComponent** and **memoization**.
- o You also learned about **memory management, background tasks**, and how to handle **local storage** using **AsyncStorage, SQLite**, and **Realm**.

4. **Testing and Debugging**:

- o We delved into testing strategies, including **unit testing with Jest, UI testing with Detox**, and **end-to-end testing with Appium**.
- o You also learned debugging techniques, such as using **Chrome Developer Tools, React Native Debugger**, and **Performance Monitors** to resolve issues efficiently.

5. **Deploying Your App**:

- You gained a solid understanding of how to **prepare your app for production**, including generating app icons and splash screens, configuring build settings, and ensuring that your app meets **App Store** and **Google Play** guidelines.
- The chapter on **deploying to the App Store and Google Play** taught you the step-by-step process of submitting your app for review, preparing necessary assets, and handling app updates and versioning.

6. **Keeping Up with the Ecosystem**:

- You explored how to stay up-to-date with the latest tools and libraries in the React Native ecosystem, including how to leverage community resources for ongoing learning and support.

By the end of this book, you should feel comfortable building, deploying, and maintaining React Native apps with confidence. Whether you're working on a personal project or joining a development team, you now have the foundational knowledge to take your skills to the next level.

Encouragement for Continued Learning and Practice

The journey to mastering React Native doesn't stop here. While this book has provided a comprehensive introduction to React

Native, becoming proficient with any technology requires continued practice and learning. Here are some ways to continue your development:

1. **Build More Apps**: The best way to learn and improve your React Native skills is by building apps. Don't be afraid to experiment with different types of apps and features. Building small projects, like a weather app or a note-taking app, will help solidify your knowledge and give you hands-on experience.

2. **Explore Advanced Topics**: As you become more comfortable with React Native, consider diving deeper into advanced topics like:

   o **Native Modules**: Learn how to write custom native code in Swift, Objective-C, Java, or Kotlin to extend React Native functionality.

   o **Performance Optimization**: Explore deeper optimizations like **lazy loading**, **code splitting**, and **image optimization**.

   o **React Native Architecture**: Gain an understanding of the inner workings of React Native, such as the bridge, native code integration, and performance bottlenecks.

3. **Contribute to Open Source**: The React Native community is vibrant and open-source contributions are a great way to give back. Consider contributing to existing libraries or building your own tools that solve common

problems faced by developers. Open source contributions are also a great way to learn from other experienced developers and improve your coding practices.

4. **Stay Updated**: React Native is constantly evolving, with frequent updates and new features being released. Stay updated by following React Native's official blog, GitHub repository, and community forums. Attend conferences and meetups to network with other React Native developers.

Ideas for Future App Projects to Expand Your Skills

Once you're comfortable with the basics of React Native, here are some app project ideas that will challenge you and help expand your skills:

1. **E-commerce App**: Build a fully-functional e-commerce app where users can browse products, add items to their cart, and complete purchases. You'll work with complex UI elements, state management, and integrating APIs for payments (e.g., Stripe or PayPal).

2. **Social Media App**: Build a social media app where users can sign up, post updates, like and comment on posts, and follow other users. This will challenge your skills in working with real-time data, authentication, and user-generated content.

3. **Fitness Tracking App**: Create a fitness tracking app that allows users to track their workouts, set goals, and monitor progress. You'll need to integrate sensors and APIs for step counting, workout logging, and possibly even video integration for workout guides.

4. **News Reader App**: Develop a news reader app that pulls articles from an API (e.g., NewsAPI or RSS feeds) and presents them in an easy-to-read format. You'll gain experience in API integration, pagination, and display optimization for large lists of data.

5. **Real-Time Collaboration App**: Build a real-time collaboration app where users can work on documents or projects simultaneously. Use Firebase or WebSockets for real-time updates and implement collaborative features like live editing and chat.

6. **Food Delivery App**: Develop a food delivery app where users can browse restaurants, order food, track delivery, and pay. This project will teach you how to integrate maps, geolocation, and payments into your app.

7. **Multimedia Streaming App**: Build a multimedia streaming app where users can watch videos or listen to music. This will help you explore working with media files, streaming services, and offline content caching.

8. **Augmented Reality (AR) App**: Use libraries like **React Native AR** or **ViroReact** to build an augmented reality

app. This project will introduce you to AR development and integration in React Native.

Conclusion

Congratulations on completing this book! You've now gained the foundational skills needed to build, deploy, and optimize React Native apps. But remember, mastering any technology is a continuous process. Keep building projects, learning new concepts, and engaging with the React Native community to stay ahead of the curve. Whether you're working on small personal projects or contributing to larger open-source applications, the opportunities are endless.

Good luck on your React Native journey, and keep coding!

www.ingramcontent.com/pod-product-compliance
Lightning Source LLC
LaVergne TN
LVHW022337060326
832902LV00022B/4093